A WORD FOR YOUR SEASON

STRATEGIES FOR RECOGNIZING AND
PURPOSEFULLY NAVIGATING THE FOUR
SPIRITUAL SEASONS EMBEDDED IN 2
TIMOTHY 3:16

JOY JOSHUA

COPYRIGHT

A Word for Your Season

Strategies for Recognizing and Purposefully

Navigating the Four Spiritual Seasons embedded in 2 Timothy 3:16

© 2025 by Joy Joshua

"To everything there is a season, and a time to every purpose under the heaven"

Ecclesiastes 3:1 (KJV)

Dedicated

To the beauty of my life, my Maker who loves me
unconditionally.

And

To my son who rises and overcomes every adversity
with the purest of faith.

Table of Contents

CHAPTER ONE

INTRODUCTION

You may wonder how this book came to be—let me explain.
After 12 years of marriage and five separations, I finally
decided to file for divorce. I reached a point when life no
longer held clear meaning and was devoid of direction. It felt
like I kept going around the same mountain repeatedly. One
morning, I came to the realization that my circumstances
had significantly deteriorated, leaving me solely responsible
for managing the situation—or so it initially appeared. I
began to question my faith and give God a side eye
wondering how in the world all these trials will work out for
my good. We both entered the marriage with the expectation
that it would be permanent; divorce was never a possibility in
our minds. However, challenges such as miscarriages, an
affair, betrayal, deception, deaths, rejection, abandonment,
and heartaches can leave behind unresolved conflicts that
then undermine the relationship. Following the tragedies, we
struggled to communicate our grief; this led to feelings of
isolation while the affair introduced a layer of betrayal that
eroded trust and sense of security.

We had completed a major relocation to another part of the
country. Just as we were settling into our new routines—my
son adjusting to unfamiliar faces at school and me
navigating the uncertainties of a different workplace, I
learned my husband had a yearlong affair that might have
resulted in a child. The revelation shattered any sense of

stability we had begun to build. The world seemed to tilt beneath my feet. I recall getting into my car driving, sobbing and yelling out my frustrations at God. I spent most nights sobbing into my pillow until my eyes burned and my chest ached. The silence of the new house felt like heavy weight pressing in around me. Everything I knew and held dear was stripped away, leaving me adrift in a sea of disbelief and heartbreak.

As an ER nurse with a school-age child, I had to quickly move past my grief and stay strong due to the demands of work and parenting. I forgave without being asked, seeking peace of mind and answered prayers. Did Jesus not say to forgive seventy-seven time? I decided to maintain composure and perseverance, continued to keep the faith despite experiencing harassment from his former partner. I maintained a consistent routine of attending church with my child to provide a sense of stability and normalcy. On one such occasion during a Bible study session, we were discussing 2 Timothy 3:16-17 (KJV):

> *"All scripture is given by inspiration of God, and is <u>profitable</u> for doctrine, for reproof, for correction, for instruction in righteousness: [17] That the man of God may be perfect, thoroughly furnished unto all good works."*

I have read this scripture many times over the years but that day, I saw it differently. All I could hear in my spirit was, "seasons, you are in a new season, and the inspired word of God is profitable (has a purpose) for every season, including the present season."

All scripture is given by _Inspiration_ – meaning the drawing in of breath. The Holy Spirit is referred to as the breath of God.

And when he had said this, he breathed on them, and saith unto them, Receive ye the Holy Ghost:
John 20:22 (KJV)

The writers of the word of God received the breath of God to write events that happened before their time. The book of Genesis is attributed to Moses who was not present during creation. The inspired word of God is _"profitable"_ – the Greek word is **ophelimos** meaning helpful, serviceable, advantageous. Helpful means giving aid or assistance. The word of God is my advantage for **every** season that I go through. The word of God is divinely breathed by the Holy Spirit (our helper) to help us, to provide us with assistance in every season.

I asked the Lord to reveal my current season, wishing to understand how His word might serve me during this period. I needed a personal word from God, I could feel myself drying up from the inside out. I needed the sustaining power of God's word to make sense of my life and to stay afloat. I stared at 2 Timothy 3:16-17 scripture and meditated on it the next couple days. It pierced through my soul and quickened something in me that I could not shake off. I gained a clearer understanding of what Jeremiah meant when he said,

⁹ Then I said, I will not make mention of him, nor speak any more in his name. But his word was in mine heart as a burning fire shut up in my bones, and I was weary with forbearing, and I could not stay. Jeremiah 20:9 (KJV)

I recognized that I was experiencing a period marked by dryness, lack of hope, and absence of affection. This became even more evident to me when my interactions with others felt distant and mechanical. I became a shadow of my former self and as an introvert, I tried keeping to myself and avoided mentioning or praising God while dealing with my grief. When I did that, I felt more pain, more restlessness, more uneasy. It only deepened my grief and discomfort. In my job, I witnessed pain daily and I could not remain indifferent to others' struggles. Even when I lacked hope, I still spoke words of encouragement to others. I was reminded of the scripture:

8 But what saith it? The word is nigh thee, even in thy mouth, and in thy heart: that is, the word of faith, which we preach;
Romans 10:8 (KJV)

Although I possessed knowledge of the word and was able to articulate it and motivate others with its message, I struggled with fully embracing and believing it for myself. I felt isolated and fearful of the distant future. My prayers were mostly filled with tears and mumbling. I asked, "why me" repeatedly. I sought healing for my broken heart and prayed for joy to come speedily but there was no escaping the pain of betrayal. I still don't know how I made it through day to day. When you are filled with the word of God, even when you least expect it, it comes to anchor your faith to help you weather through a stormy season.

It was during that period of brokenness that God opened my eyes to see the four seasons outlined in 2 Timothy 3:16 – the season of doctrine, season of reproof, season of correction, and the season of instruction in righteousness. How:

- We must first identify our current season
- Understand its specific requirements
- Determine what actions are necessary to meet those unique demands,
- And apply the strategies outlined in His word to successfully navigate through it and come out victorious.

The word of God is helpful to us in every season. By studying the scriptures, we can identify individuals who experienced similar seasons, examine the actions they took to address the demands of that season, and adopt their successful strategies when appropriate. We gain valuable insights from the examples set by saints recorded in the Bible; their lives were documented to provide guidance and inspiration for future generations. There are no short cuts with God, He is interested in who we are and not in what we do. In our part of the world, we experience Winter, Spring, Summer, and Fall each year, dressing for the weather—shorts in summer and warm clothes in winter. As one season concludes, another commences—an ongoing pattern observed in life. This principle can similarly be seen in the word of God. Within our spiritual development, we experience four distinct seasons: doctrine, reproof, correction, and instruction.

To everything there is a season, and a time to every purpose under the heaven".
Ecclesiastes 3:1(KJV)

Season is an appointed occasion, an appointed time, a set time. To everything there is a set time, an appointed time – a time decided beforehand for every purpose under heaven. Keeping this in mind during life's difficulties or challenges may lead to a different perspective or shift in thinking.

The question changes from "when is this going to end?" to "how is this going to end?" The "when" is given, we know it will end because it was decided beforehand. A time was set for that life change, that betrayal, that sickness, that victory, that healing, that childbirth, that miscarriage and everything else in-between for a season.

> ²² *While the earth remaineth, seedtime and harvest, and cold and heat, and summer and winter, and day and night shall not cease.*
> **Genesis 8:22 (KJV)**

Will it end? Yes, when? At the appointed time. How will it end? It depends on what you do with the season you are in.

I inquired of the Holy Spirit regarding the current season in which I find myself. His answer was to take me to 1 Chronicles 12:32 (KJV)

> ³² *And of the children of Issachar, which were men that had understanding of the times, to know what Israel ought to do; the heads of them were two hundred; and all their brethren were at their commandment.*

Et is the Hebrew word for time meaning occurrence, occasion, season.

The sons of Issachar had understanding (discernment, knowledge, wisdom) of the times (season), to know (perceive, instruct, tell, teach, discern, discover) what Israel ought to do. Their understanding of the season positioned them to instruct, to teach Israel what to do.

Seasons are discerned with wisdom and understanding. What is discernment?

The dictionary definition of discernment is the ability to judge well, the quality of being able to grasp and comprehend what is obscure.

How do I obtain discernment?

2 And be not conformed to this world: but be ye transformed by the renewing (renovation, complete change for the better) of your mind, that ye may prove (discern) what is that good, and acceptable, and perfect, will of God.

Romans 12:2 (KJV)

We obtain discernment through mind renewal. We renew our minds by replacing our old way of thinking with the word of God, then we can discern the will of God for our lives and be able to judge well and make sound decisions.

7 Wisdom is the principal (the first, best, chief, choice part) thing; therefore get wisdom: and with all thy getting get understanding (discernment). 8 Exalt her (esteem highly), and she shall promote thee: she shall bring thee to honour, when thou dost embrace her.
Proverbs 4:7-8

Wisdom (the first, best, chief, choice part) and understanding (discernment) help us avoid repeating the same mistakes and allow us to move forward. It costs us nothing to obtain wisdom. God offers it freely to anyone who would ask.

> [5] *If any of you lacks wisdom, you should ask God, who gives generously to all without finding fault, and it will be given to you.*
> **James 1:5 (NIV)**

I occasionally struggle with asking, and I recognize the need for personal improvement in this area. We serve a God who sits in the heavens and makes the earth his footstool, the earth and everything in it belongs to him. Yet we sometimes limit him.

> *You do not have because you do not ask God.*
> **James 4:2b (NIV)**

There's no harm in asking; the worst outcome is a "no" or "wait." But what if He says yes? Upon further reflection, I recognized that the experiences of rejection and abandonment throughout the years contributed to a sense of unworthiness regarding receiving attention and love from God. These experiences influenced and negatively affected my perception of God. I unconsciously began to see God as only willing to meet my needs and not my wants. As I write this book, I am relearning how to ask my father, our heavenly father, for everything I want. I want love, joy, I want to be happy again, to laugh again, to be whole. I know He can meet those needs and more because He can do exceedingly abundantly above all that we ask or think, according to the power that worketh in us (Ephesians 3:20)

Challenge yourself to start asking your father for everything you need and want. My child makes various requests; for some, I agree, for others, I decline, and some I postpone for further consideration. We have got to stop adulting for a change and start going to God like a child.

³ and said, "I assure you and most solemnly say to you, unless you repent [that is, change your inner self—your old way of thinking, live changed lives] and become like children [trusting, humble, and forgiving], you will never enter the kingdom of heaven.
Matthew 18:3 (AMP)

Please note: Diamond bullets in this book are used to highlight or summarize the main purpose of each season.

CHAPTER TWO

THE SEASON OF DOCTRINE IN RIGHTEOUSNESS

*"All scripture is given by inspiration of God, and is profitable for **doctrine,** for reproof, for correction, for instruction in righteousness: [17] That the man of God may be perfect, thoroughly furnished unto all good works.*

2 Timothy 3:16-17 (KJV)

The Greek word for doctrine is ***didaskalia*** meaning learning, teaching. The dictionary definition of learning is the acquisition of knowledge or skills through experience, study, or by being taught. Teaching is defined as the process of sharing knowledge with others. Only a person with a teachable heart can learn. When we think we have things already figured out, we're not teachable.

"Study to shew thyself approved unto God, a workman that needeth not to be ashamed, rightly dividing the word of truth.
2 Timothy 2:15 (KJV)

To rightly divide the word or to accurately handle the word is the Greek word **Orthotomeo** – to make straight and smooth, to dissect, to teach the truth directly and correctly. You dissect the word to acquire knowledge, and you impart the knowledge you received truthfully and correctly.

- *The doctrine season is our season of acquiring knowledge of the word with a teachable spirit and a willingness to share the knowledge we have received with others.*

We all begin our spiritual journey in the foundational season of doctrine as new followers of Christ. We enter the Christian faith eager to learn, like newborns craving nourishment that is essential for our spiritual growth.

² like newborn babies [you should] long for the pure milk of the word, so that by it you may be nurtured and grow in respect to salvation [its ultimate fulfillment],
1 Peter 2:2

Why do we need to acquire the knowledge of the word of God? Jesus said to his disciples in John 16:33 (KJV):

³³ These things I have spoken unto you, that in me ye might have peace. In the world ye shall have tribulation: but be of good cheer; I have <u>overcome</u> the world.

He stated that we will experience tribulation—***thlipsis*** in Greek, referring to persecution, affliction, oppression, or trouble—in this world. This message most likely caused concern among the disciples when they heard it. Thankfully He goes on to say, "but take courage I have overcome the world." To overcome – *nikao* is to conquer, to come off victorious, to prevail, carry off the victory.

⁵ And one of the elders saith unto me, Weep not: behold, the Lion of the tribe of Judah, the Root of David, hath <u>prevailed</u> to open the book, and to loose the seven seals thereof.
Revelation 5:5 (KJV)

Do not sob, do not mourn, be of good courage the lion of the tribe of Judah hath prevailed – same Greek word *nikao* (to conquer, to come off victorious, to overcome, carry off the victory), glory to God. He prevailed when He overcame the enemy with the word in the wilderness after forty days and forty nights of fasting, He prevailed when he disarmed principalities and powers, He made a public spectacle of them, triumphing over them by the cross (Colossians 2:15). He crushed our common enemy's head. We need to know the word of God Because a time is coming when persecution or trouble will arise because of the word. Look at Mark 4:17 (NIV) –

¹⁷ But since they have no root, they last only a short time. <u>When</u> trouble or persecution comes<u> because of the word</u>, they quickly fall away.

"When" is the key word here not **if**, meaning trouble will come. Trials and tribulation are to be expected, and we are to face them with courage because we can overcome them.

[11] And they <u>overcame</u> (nikao)him by the blood of the Lamb, and by the word of their testimony; and they loved not their lives unto the death.
Revelation 12:11(KJV)

They <u>overcame</u> (the same Greek word **nikao** referring to conquer, to come off victorious, to prevail, carry off the victory) with the blood of Jesus and the <u>word</u> (**logos** – the word of God, the sayings of God). Jesus overcame the enemy so that we can overcome with His blood and His word.

When trouble comes if we are not rooted in the word we will quickly fall away. To quickly fall away is the Greek word **skandalizo – (***think of scandal and you will remember this word)* – entrap, trip up, fall, be enticed to sin, be offended.

We often reach out to others for support, prayer, or advice during difficult times, but we sometimes struggle to settle down and study the Bible—our instruction manual for daily living that helps keep us from falling into temptation. Think about what we do when our Wi-Fi suddenly disconnects: we reach for the manual, walk through the troubleshooting steps, and sometimes all it takes is unplugging and plugging the router back in to restore the connection.

 In the same way, when trials and tribulations arise, instead of panicking or seeking immediate outside help it is important to return to fundamental principles by disconnecting from external distractions, including social media and public opinion, and plug into the power of God's word. We can turn to the Bible for practical guidance and solutions. Just as the Wi-Fi manual can help us restore our internet connection, the Bible—through prayer—can help us reset and reconnect with God. Our individual journey is unique and God's expression in us is equally unique, not like any other. We troubleshoot by studying the word of God, fasting and praying to seek the expertise of our manufacturer – God.

The doctrine season holds significant importance for the following reasons:

1. It is necessary for hydration.

"Jesus answered and said unto her, If thou knewest the gift of God, and who it is that saith to thee, give me to drink; thou wouldest have asked of him, and he would have given thee living water".
John 4:10 (KJV)

In the biblical account from John 4, the Samaritan woman meets Jesus at Jacob's well—a place she visited daily to satisfy her physical thirst. Yet, beneath the surface, she carried a deeper longing, her soul parched by disappointment and unmet needs. She had experienced the pain of broken relationships, having had five husbands and now living with a man who was not her husband, still searching for fulfillment. The things she clung to—love, acceptance, companionship—never truly satisfied her heart, instead they left her feeling empty and alone. In this vulnerable moment, her thirst was not just for water, but for hope and meaning that seemed out of reach. Until that moment arrived when her footsteps were ordered to meet the living water face to face.

I can certainly relate with this woman. I found myself in that place of extreme thirst and desperation for a personal word from my Savior. I needed just one word to unlock the channel of living water within. I had gotten so used to pouring into everybody else that I neglected myself, giving and serving until I was running on empty. During those years, I often felt isolated, weary, and unsure if I would ever feel whole again; spiritual dryness became my normal, and I carried that weight with quiet resignation.

When I finally came to the living spring, much like the Samaritan woman, I didn't know how to receive or even recognize the refreshment offered to me. But as I opened my heart and let God's word speak to me, I began to feel the slow but steady flow of living water washing over my soul, bringing restoration where there had been exhaustion and emptiness.

But whosoever drinketh of the water that I shall give him shall never thirst; but the water that I shall give him shall be in him a well of water springing up into everlasting life. ¹⁵ The woman saith unto him, Sir, give me this water, that I thirst not, neither come hither to draw.
John 4:14-15 (KJV)

The conversation at the well opened the flood gate of salvation that flooded not only her life but the life of everyone in her city. Her thirst became the conduit of change. Do not underestimate the power of your thirst. It can drive you to your knees, it can push you to desperation and desperation if channeled in the right direction can result in the salvation of many. We know that the Samaritan woman - this nameless woman, known only by the name of her city became the first evangelist in the New Testament right after hydrating from the spring of living water. The moment she drank the water of His word, a well of living water sprang up within her and overflowed to her city. Out of her dryness, hunger and desire for spiritual hydration came the salvation of her city.

"Everyone who thirsts, come to the waters;
And you who have no money come, buy grain and eat.
Come, buy wine and milk
Without money and without cost [simply accept it as a gift
from God].
Isaiah 55:1

When we commit to the season of learning, we are committing ourselves to being refreshed daily. Who knows how many lives we can change starting from our home if we take the time to sit at the feet of our Savior and drink from His word just like Mary, the sister of Lazarus.

2. **It is necessary for our sanctification and cleansing.**

[25] Husbands, love your wives, even as Christ also loved the church, and gave himself for it; [26] That he might sanctify and cleanse it with the washing of water by the word, [27] That he might present it to himself a glorious church, not having spot, or wrinkle, or any such thing; but that it should be holy and without blemish.
Ephesians 5:25-27 (KJV)

Sanctify means to consecrate oneself to God, to be set apart for a special purpose, to make holy. To cleanse is to purify, to be free from defilement of sin and from faults.

The word of God cleanses and frees us from the defilement of sin. The writer of *Psalm 119:9 (NKJV) said,*

> *"How can a young man cleanse his way? By taking <u>heed</u> according to Your word"*

To take heed is the Hebrew word **samar** – meaning to keep the word, retain the word, treasure up the word of God (in memory). When the word of God leaps off the pages of the bible and takes residence in our heart, it rules our life and keeps us from falling into sin.

Psalm 119 writer goes further to say in verse 11:

> *"Your word I have <u>hidden</u> in my heart, That I might not sin against You".*

Sapan is the Hebrew word hidden – to treasure, to store, to reserve, to protect, to keep secretly. The Psalmist knew that the heart is desperately wicked (Jeremiah 17:9) and that as a man thinketh in his heart so is he (one and the same), he decided to stay ahead of the game by storing up on the word of God to keep him from sin. The Psalmist chose to stay prepared, refusing to let the enemy catch him off guard. This is living intentionally. Another person who chose to live prepared is Job. He said in chapter 23:12 (NKJV)

> *[12] I have not departed from the commandment of His lips; I have <u>treasured</u> the words of His mouth More than my necessary food.*

The word treasured is the same Hebrew word **sapan** to store up. Job made storing the word more priority than food. At the start of the COVID pandemic, those who closely followed the news and understood the situation stocked up on food, toilet paper, and other essentials. When the pandemic ended, friends I know built a second pantry and started storing for another pandemic/natural disaster, they did not want to be caught off guard again. They began to prepare for life with the same foresight shown by the five wise virgins, who brought additional oil in readiness for the arrival of the bridegroom. When the bridegroom delayed his coming, their lamps went off during the night. The foolish virgins did not have oil to replenish their lamps and so they missed the bridegrooms. Joseph advised Pharoh to store up food in the time of plenty to prepare for years of famine.

[45] A good man brings good things out of the good stored up in his heart, and an evil man brings evil things out of the evil stored up in his heart. For the mouth speaks what the heart is full of.
Luke 6:45 (NIV)

What we store up in our heart is what we will speak, and what we speak will set the course of our life.

3. It is necessary for warfare.

[11] Put on the full armor of God, so that you can take your stand against the devil's schemes.
Ephesians 6:11 (NIV)

Verse 14-18 list the full armor of God – the belt of truth, the breastplate of righteousness, feet strapped with the gospel of peace, the shield of faith, the helmet of salvation, the sword of the Spirit which is the word of God and pray in the Spirit on all occasions with all kinds of prayers and requests.

The sword of the Spirit which is the word of God is the only amour of God that we have that is a weapon of offense. The other armors are all for defense. When David was going to face Goliath, King Saul dressed him in his armor. David tried walking around with them, but he could not use King Saul's coat of armor in battle because he was not used to them, he had never battled with them. He had practiced facing his adversaries in the past with God, a sling and some smooth stones. When it was time to face the giant, he could not risk battling with an armor that was foreign to him.

God has given us His full armor. God is not asking us to wear an armor that He has not used. In Isaiah 59:17 God put on his armor to battle His enemies – same armor that He gave us.

17 He put on righteousness as his breastplate, and the helmet of salvation on his head; he put on the garments of vengeance and wrapped himself in zeal as in a cloak.
18 According to what they have done, so will he repay wrath to his enemies and retribution to his foes; he will repay the islands their due.
Isaiah 59:17 (NIV)

If it is necessary even for God to don armor in preparation for battle, then it is essential that we, too, equip ourselves appropriately. When the devil tempted Jesus three times in the wilderness in Matthew 4:1-11, Jesus countered with "it is written." He used his word – the sword of the Spirit against the devil with each temptation.

1st Temptation: *Then Jesus was led by the Spirit into the wilderness to be tempted by the devil. ² After fasting forty days and forty nights, he was hungry. ³ The tempter came to him and said, "If you are the Son of God, tell these stones to become bread."*

⁴ Jesus answered, **"It is written***: 'Man shall not live on bread alone, but on every word that comes from the mouth of God.'"*

2nd Temptation: *⁵ Then the devil took him to the holy city and had him stand on the highest point of the temple. ⁶ "If you are the Son of God," he said, "throw yourself down. For it is written:*

"'He will command his angels concerning you, and they will lift you up in their hands, so that you will not strike your foot against a stone."

⁷ Jesus answered him, **"It is also written***: 'Do not put the Lord your God to the test."*

3rd Temptation: *⁸ ⁸ Again, the devil took him to a very high mountain and showed him all the kingdoms of the world and their splendor. ⁹ "All this I will give you," he said, "if you will bow down and worship me."*

¹⁰ Jesus said to him, "Away from me, Satan! **For it is written***: 'Worship the Lord your God, and serve him only"*

¹¹ Then the devil left him, and angels came and attended him.
Matthew 4:1-11(NIV)

The angels came and attended to Jesus. The word attend is the Greek word **diakoneo** meaning to minister, to serve, to wait upon at a table and offer food and drink to the guests. Jesus had fasted for 40 days and 40 nights and he was hungry. Satan was aware of this and tempted him with food while the angels waited in the wings with bated breath with food and succor for him. Jesus did not give in to the momentary hunger, because what was to come was greater. After overcoming the temptation, Jesus went forward to choose the twelve disciples.

Remember that our common enemy, the devil also knows the word of God, he said to Jesus in Matthew chapter 4:6,

⁶ "If you are the Son of God," he said, "throw yourself down. **For it is written***:*

"'He will command his angels concerning you,
and they will lift you up in their hands,
so that you will not strike your foot against a stone."
Matthew 4:6 (NIV)

The devil said to Jesus, the angels will come to attend to you if you throw yourself down. But Jesus did not give in to him, and the angels still came to attend to Jesus. Jesus used the word of God to overcome the devil. Hide the word in your heart, store it up, reserve it, protect it. If you do, you will spot the deception of the enemy from afar off. He sought out Eve in the garden and deceived her. He knows how to get us to the place of questioning what God already told us to do or to twist the word of God. Did God really say to do so and so?

The devil has no new tricks; he continues to employ the same weapon of deception that he has used throughout history. When King Hezekiah faced King Sennacherib of Assyria in 2 Kings 18, Sennacherib employed the art of lies and deception in his battle against Judah. Sennacherib had conquered Israel for disobeying God and then he advanced against Judah. But Judah had righteous Hezekiah as their King and he did what was right in the eyes of God. Rabshakeh – Sennacherib's spokesman came with a great army and said to the people in 2nd Kings 18:25 that God sent him to destroy Judah.

25 Am I now come up without the LORD against this place to destroy it? The LORD said to me, go up against this land, and destroy it.
2 Kings 18:25(KJV)

Hearing these words must have made the people of Judah fearful and to question if God was for them. But Rabshakeh did not stop there, he continues in verse 31-36 (KJV):

31 Hearken not to Hezekiah: for thus saith the king of Assyria, Make an agreement with me by a present, and come out to me, and then eat ye every man of his own vine, and every one of his fig tree, and drink ye every one the waters of his cistern:

³² Until I come and take you away to a land like your own land, a land of corn and wine, a land of bread and vineyards, a land of oil olive and of honey, that ye may live, and not die: and hearken not unto Hezekiah, when he persuadeth you, saying, The LORD will deliver us.

³³ Hath any of the gods of the nations delivered at all his land out of the hand of the king of Assyria? ³⁴ Where are the gods of Hamath, and of Arpad? where are the gods of Sepharvaim, Hena, and Ivah? have they delivered Samaria out of mine hand?

³⁵ Who are they among all the gods of the countries, that have delivered their country out of mine hand, that the LORD should deliver Jerusalem out of mine hand?

³⁶ But the people held their peace, and answered him not a word: for the king's commandment was, saying, Answer him not.
2 Kings 18:31-36 (KJV)

Sennacherib lied that God sent him to destroy Judah, he asked them to make peace with him, that he would take them to a land **like** their land, that God would not deliver them from his hand. Just like the devil, he comes in, walks around like a roaring lion looking for whom to devour, looking to catch us off guard. Like in the parable of the Sower,

[24] Another parable put he forth unto them, saying, The kingdom of heaven is likened unto a man which sowed good seed in his field: [25] But <u>while men slept</u>, his enemy came and sowed tares among the wheat, and went his way.
Matthew 13:24-25 (KJV)

Do not be caught off guard. Do not spend your time sleeping. Wake up sleeper. When the devil tells you that you are all alone without help, tell him 'I am onto your lies and deception, for it is written in *Hebrews 13:5b –6 (NIV):*

"Never will I leave you; never will I forsake you." [6] So we say with confidence, "The Lord is my helper; I will not be afraid. What can mere mortals do to me?"

Always counter the enemy with the word of God, it is one of the weapons of our warfare that is mighty through the Holy ghost to the pulling down of strongholds. Practice wielding the sword of the Spirit (the word of God) ensuring that you are well-prepared and familiar with it, so that during times of spiritual battle it will not be foreign to you. When is the time of war? Now, we are constantly battling an enemy.

So, take everything the Master has set out for you, well-made weapons of the best materials. And put them to use so you will be able to stand up to everything the Devil throws your way. <u>This is no weekend war</u> that we'll walk away from and forget about in a couple of hours. This is for keeps, a life-or-death fight to the finish against the Devil and all his angels.
Ephesians 6:11-12 (The Message)

4. It is necessary for prosperity.

Moses, who led the Israelites (the man who parted the Red Sea), had recently passed away, after which Joshua assumed leadership of Israel. Joshua faced high expectations and likely doubted his suitability for the role. He was probably terrified, but God encountered Joshua with the intention of providing motivation, encouragement and all he needed to succeed in his new position.

⁷Only be strong and very courageous; be careful to do [everything] in accordance with the entire law which Moses My servant commanded you; do not turn from it to the right or to the left, so that you may prosper and be successful wherever you go. ⁸This book of the Law shall not depart from your mouth, but you shall read (and meditate on) it day and night, so that you may be careful to do (everything) in accordance with all that is written in it, for then you will make your way prosperous, and then you will be successful.

Joshua 1:7-8 (AMP)

The word prosperous in Hebrew is **sakal** meaning prosper, prudent, circumspect, understanding, skill, teach, wise, instruct – all the qualities Joshua needed to possess to be a great leader. God pretty much laid it all out for Joshua. He told him his success is contingent on obeying the entire law and gave him the key to prosperity. God is saying the ball is in your courts, you will make your own way prosperous by speaking my word, meditating on my word, and obeying my word. Prosperity in this verse is conditioned on these three steps: Speak, meditate and obey in that order. Without studying, speaking, pondering, mediating on God's word, it would be difficult to remember and obey it. How will you obey the word you do not know?

²² Do not merely listen to the word, and so deceive yourselves. Do what it says. ²³ Anyone who listens to the word but does not do what it says is like someone who looks at his face in a mirror ²⁴ and, after looking at himself, goes away and immediately forgets what he looks like. ²⁵ But whoever looks intently into the perfect law that gives freedom, and continues in it—not forgetting what they have heard, but doing it—they will be blessed in what they do.

James 1:22-25(NIV)

James is saying that if we listen to the word and obey the word, we will be blessed - to be well off, fortunate, happy.

Both scriptures give us the key to success. God is not asking us as believers to perform his word, that's his job. All He is looking for is our obedience to His word. When we obey His word, we come into partnership with Him to bring His kingdom and will on earth as it is in heaven.

And Samuel said, Hath the LORD as great delight in burnt offerings and sacrifices, as in obeying the voice of the LORD? Behold, to obey is better than sacrifice, and to hearken than the fat of rams.
1 Samuel 15:22 (KJV)

During my study, I found that the word "obey" in this context is translated from the Hebrew word **sama**, which can also mean to consent or agree. Consent means to give permission for something to happen.

When we obey God, we are agreeing with His will and giving Him permission to use us to accomplish His will on earth.

We see Mary consenting to carry the Savior in her womb, all she did was utter these words,

> *"And Mary said, Behold the handmaid of the Lord; be it unto me according to thy word. And the angel departed from her"*
> **Luke 1:38 (KJV)**

God performed what she agreed to. Elijah agreed in prayer with God to send the rain after God had promised to send rain on the land.

> *And it came to pass after many days, that the word of the Lord came to Elijah in the third year, saying, Go, shew thyself unto Ahab; and I will send rain upon the earth.*
> **1 Kings 18:1(KJV)**

God said he will send rain, Elijah prayed in obedience to His word.

> *Elijah was a human being, even as we are. He prayed earnestly that it would not rain, and it did not rain on the land for three and a half years. [18] Again he prayed, and the heavens gave rain, and the earth produced its crops.*
> **James 5:17-18 (NIV)**

♦ *Our obedience is our consent/agreement to see the will of our father done in our lives, in our homes, jobs, communities etc.*

¹² Then the Lord said to me, "You have seen well, for I am [actively] watching over My word to <u>fulfill</u> it."
Jeremiah 1:12 (AMP)

So shall my word be that goeth forth out of my mouth: it shall not return unto me void, but it shall <u>accomplish</u> that which I please, and it shall prosper in the thing whereto I sent it.
Isaiah 55:11 (KJV)

The words fulfill and accomplish is the same Hebrew word **asa** meaning to do, to work, execute, perform, to bring to pass. We obey and God works His word. The same way that God wants our obedience - our consent, our partnership, our agreement is the same way that the devil also seeks our consent/obedience. In 2 Kings 18:31 (KJV), Sennacherib asked Judah to make an agreement with him, to allow him to invade their land.

³¹ Hearken not to Hezekiah: for thus saith the king of Assyria, Make an agreement with me by a present, and come out to me, and then eat ye every man of his own vine, and every one of his fig tree, and drink ye every one the waters of his cistern:

Why did he need their consent to invade their land? We are slaves to whoever we choose to obey. James in chapter 1 suggests that reading the word of God alone is insufficient; we must also do it, obey it, consent or agree with it to experience its associated benefits. We must continuously monitor our eye gate (what we see), our ear gate (what we hear), our mouth gate (what we speak), our mind gate (what we think on) to prevent the enemy from gaining access. Paul in Ephesians 4:8 gave us a list of things to think about – TRN APPLE was the acronym I was taught in college to assist in recalling these. Whatsoever things that are true, right, noble, admirable, pure, praiseworthy, lovely and excellent, think on these things.

If we focus on God's word—by reading, listening, speaking, and meditating on it—we align ourselves spiritually to follow His teachings and take territories for Him.

5. It is necessary for illumination.

In the beginning God created the heavens and the earth. ²
Now the earth was formless and empty, darkness was over
the surface of the deep, and the Spirit of God was hovering
over the waters. ³ And God said, "Let there be light," and
there was light.
Genesis 1:1-3 (NIV)

The Hebrew word for light is **or** pronounced ore, it refers to illumination. The definition for illumination is to make (something) visible or bright by shining light on it, make (something) known to humans by divine help, to clarify or explain something by providing further information about it. Its opposite is to conceal or confuse.

The Hebrew word *or* was present in the beginning when God created the world. We see the Spirit of God hovering over the waters after God had made the heavens and the earth. The earth was without form (Hebrew word *to-hoo*) meaning formlessness, unreal, emptiness, confusion, chaos, wilderness, nothing, waste and dark (obscure). From hovering over the waters, He calls out to God, "it's too dark out here, we need to see what we are working with." Then God said, "let there be light."

Light did not show up until God spoke. His word brought light which made what was invisible visible, it formed what was formless, it made what was ambiguous clear, it made the obscure transparent, it brought order to what was chaotic, it made what was unreal real, it filled the void. God then goes on to finish His creation.

The God of the universe needed light, and he created it. Light crowds out darkness and illuminates

Thy word is a lamp unto my feet, and a light unto my path.
Psalm 119:105 (KJV)

Your word, Hebrew word – *dabar* (commandment, acts, chronicles) is a light or illumination to my pathway. It can make our pathway visible; it can provide us with clarity.

♦ *God's word can provide the clarity we need to make good decision.*

What are you going through that looks insurmountable, confusing, ambiguous? It might be that all you need is the light of God's word. Study the word, it will bring clarity, understanding, and revelation.

The entrance of thy words giveth light; it giveth understanding unto the simple.
Psalm 119:130 (KJV)

Entrance is the Hebrew word **petah** meaning opening, disclosure, doorway, unfolding. That word *petah* reminds me of the unfolding of a rose petal. A rose with closed petals evokes an air of intrigue and curiosity; as the flower opens, its full elegance and splendor become apparent. The word of God is like a closed petal, full of mystery and wonder. When we open the word of God to study it, we open the door to His will, the unfolding of His word brings light (Hebrew word **or**), it gives discernment to the simple or open minded. We receive illumination that produces understanding. Jesus said in John 6:63b (KJV):

".... the words I speak unto you, they are spirit, and they are life."

The Hebrew word for Spirit is **pneuma** referring to the third person of the triune God. The word of God is living and inspired by the Holy Spirit. The Spirit of God searches the mind of God to reveal to us what God has freely given to us.

[10] these are the things God has revealed to us by his Spirit. The Spirit searches all things, even the deep things of God. [11] For who knows a person's thoughts except their own spirit within them? In the same way no one knows the thoughts of God except the Spirit of God.
1 Corinthians 2:10-11 (NIV)

The Spirit of God gives us understanding of God's word.

But there is a spirit in man, And the breath of the Almighty gives him understanding.
Job 32:8 (NKJV)

The revealed word of God brings light. For instance, I have read Isaiah 54:17 (NKJV) all my life and even sang it in a song, but one day, after facing a series of challenges that left me feeling vulnerable and uncertain, these words leaped off the pages of the Bible and came alive to me. In that moment, I realized that the promise wasn't just a general statement—it was meant for me personally, offering comfort and assurance amidst my struggles. On that particular day, I was requested to attend my son's school in response to allegations which I believed were unfounded. I sought the Lord on how to address this matter, and this verse came to mind.

"No weapon formed against me shall prosper, and every tongue which rises against you in judgment You shall condemn.
This is the heritage of the servants of the Lord, And their righteousness is from Me," Says the Lord.

To condemn is the Hebrew word ***rasa*** – means wicked, guilty, to declare wrong, to make trouble. The verse suddenly resonated in a way it never had before, filling me with hope and giving me the confidence to trust God's protection over my son's life knowing that the accusation weapon will not prosper if I condemn it, if I declare their tongue guilty and call it wrong. God has given me this promise as his servant, this is my heritage, my inheritance as His servant. My prayer suddenly had increased momentum and effectiveness.

I was able to rise and declare Isaiah 54:17 to the enemy and I went even further to let him know that it is written in Isaiah 54:13 that "all my children will be taught by the LORD, and great will be their peace."

During the doctrine season, studying, memorizing and storing the word of God in our heart will be pointless unless we remain teachable (**able to be taught**). Continuous personal growth requires an openness to learning; without a teachable mindset, we may encounter repeated challenges. The emphasis is placed on our character development and that comes from allowing the word of God to permeate us leading to a transformative change within.

God opened my eyes to see that I have spent about five years in this season, repeating the same actions and anticipating different outcomes. Isn't that insanity defined? Despite consistently obtaining various books on fostering a healthy marriage, listening to numerous marriage-focused podcasts and conferences, and sharing relevant resources with my spouse, our relationship continued to exhibit dysfunctional patterns. My efforts to learn new things were not improving my situation, and my marriage was experiencing ongoing challenges, resulting in increasing distance between us.

Being teachable gives you the ability to acquire understanding, to learn, to grow, to change.

"For whoever has a teachable heart, to him more understanding will be given; and whoever does not have a yearning for truth, even what he has will be taken away from him".
Mark 4:25 (AMP)

For a period, I lived in ignorance, and as a result, what I had was taken away from me. After losing what I had, I realized that true change starts within. This led me to reflect on the importance of self-awareness before judging others; you must first remove the log from your own eye before trying to remove the speck from another person's. You essentially become the change you want to see. For instance, when I focused on improving my own habits rather than criticizing others, I noticed positive changes not only in myself but also in my relationships. However, as I continued to acquire knowledge, I mistakenly thought I had everything figured out.

I advocated for counselling, believing it would address our issues; however, upon reflection, I recognize that part of my motivation was a desire for an external party to validate my perspective. At the time, I was not teachable, I was not receptive to personal growth, as my focus on emotional pain hindered my ability to reflect, to embrace constructive change and allow the word of God to sink in and do a healing work within me.

To learn, you must want to be taught. To refuse reproof is stupid."
Proverbs 12:1(TLB)

We perish for lack of knowledge (discernment, understanding, wisdom); therefore, it is our duty to diligently seek and acquire an understanding of God's word. For

²⁹ The secret things belong unto the LORD our God: but those things which are revealed belong unto us and to our children for ever, that we may do all the words of this law.
Deuteronomy 29:29 (KJV)

The things which are revealed – *gala* – meaning uncovered belong to us. We are responsible for searching out the word of God and for applying the knowledge we have gained to our lives. When we obey God's word and follow His principles, we position ourselves to flourish and experience true prosperity.

Does it feel like you are in a constant season of doctrine in righteousness, like you are constantly receiving knowledge, but you do not see a change in your life. Check your heart posture, are you teachable? If you do not, in the words of 2ⁿᵈ Timothy 3:7 (KJV) you will be:

"ever learning, and never able to come to the knowledge of the truth."

But hope is not lost: *"Howbeit when he, the Spirit of truth, is come, he will guide you into all truth:*
John 16:13 (KJV)

The Spirit of truth is here, surrender to His guidance.

CHAPTER THREE

THE SEASON OF REPROOF IN RIGHTEOUSNESS

*"All scripture is given by inspiration of God, and is profitable for doctrine, for **reproof,** for correction, for instruction in righteousness: ¹⁷ That the man of God may be perfect, thoroughly furnished unto all good works.*

2 Timothy 3:16-17

Reproof in Greek is **elegchos** meaning– a proof, that by which a thing is proved or tested, conviction, evidence. After acquiring knowledge of the word in the season of doctrine in righteousness, the word will undergo proving, testing in the season of reproof in righteousness.

¹³ Then Jesus said to them, "Don't you understand this parable? How then will you understand any parable? ¹⁴ The farmer sows the word. ¹⁵ Some people are like seed along the path, where the word is sown. As soon as they hear it, Satan comes and takes away the word that was sown in them. ¹⁶ Others, like seed sown on rocky places, hear the word and at once receive it with joy. ¹⁷ But since they have no root, they last only a short time. When trouble or persecution comes because of the word, they quickly fall away.

Mark 4:13-17 (NIV)

Why does Satan come after the word that was sown? Because the word produces faith in us. According to Romans 10:17 (NIV) then faith *comes* by hearing and hearing by the word of God.

- ♦ *The season of Reproof in Righteousness is the season of testing the word.*

What is faith? We all know from Hebrews 11:1 (KJV):

Now faith is the <u>substance</u> of things hoped for, the <u>evidence</u> of things not seen.

Faith is the **substance** of things hoped for.

<u>**Substance**</u> in Greek is ***hypostasis*** meaning assurance, foundation, real being, that which has actual existence.

By faith we believe that something is real before we experience it. Faith is the foundation of our Christian Walk, anything that is not done out of faith is sin according to Romans 14:23. In daily life, we routinely exercise faith, often without conscious awareness. For example, we trust that a bridge will support us when we drive across it, or that a chair will hold our weight when we sit down. We do not question the manufacturer or the engineer responsible for constructing the bridge before we use it. Instead, we simply accept that the bridge has been tested and is safe for travel.

There is no need for us to examine architectural plans or verify the credentials of the builder; we rely on what we've been told—that the bridge has passed inspection. Just as we trust experts and systems in our daily lives without direct evidence, it stands to reason that we might approach the word of God our creator with similar trust if not better.

These examples show how faith underpins much of what we do—often without hesitation. In light of this, it is worth considering how this same principle applies to matters of spirituality. If we can so readily place our faith in the words and assurances of fellow humans regarding everyday things like travel or food safety—trusting, for instance, that the food we eat is safe because the FDA has performed its due diligence—how much more might we trust the word of God, which is described as "yeah and amen"? Should we not believe it with the same, if not greater, confidence and wholeheartedness?

Faith is the **evidence** of things not seen.

Evidence in Greek is *elegchos* – this is the same word that means *Reproof*, that by which a thing is proved or tested. This blew my mind. Let us back up a bit.

2 Timothy 3:16 says the inspired word of God is profitable for Reproof. Reproof in Greek is *elegchos* a proof, that by which a thing is proved or tested.

Hebrews 11:1 says Faith is the evidence of things not seen. Evidence in Greek is also *elegchos* a proof, that by which a thing is proved or tested.

The word *Prove* is defined as to demonstrate the truth or existence of something by evidence or argument. Our faith, as evidence of the unseen, must be tested or proved.

> *[7] That the trial of your faith, being much more precious than of gold that perisheth, though it be tried with fire, might be found unto praise and honour and glory at the appearing of Jesus Christ:*
> **1 Peter 1:7 (KJV)**

Is Peter suggesting that it is not we who are being tested, but rather our faith is standing trial? If so, why? That it might be found unto praise and honor. So, when we go through trials it is not personal because we are not actually standing trial in the docket, it is our faith. The faith that can move mountains even though it is as small as a mustard seed needs to be tried.

When we for example ask God for a house, we believe for it, we pray for it, we have faith for it, we make plans for it, and we take steps towards buying one. The house is the promise we are believing for, so it becomes the "thing not seen" because it is not visible yet. Our faith is the substance, the real deal. When we finally receive the house, do we then say we have received our evidence, or have we received the promise? The evidence is not the house; our faith is the evidence. When we receive the promise which is the house, our faith (the evidence) gets stronger. Faith as small as a mustard seed can move mountains, can help us obtain the house.

If the house was the evidence, then our faith will be the "thing not seen" or the promise. But not so, faith is the substance of things hoped for, and the evidence that stood in for the thing not seen or the promise while we were believing for it. The house is the thing not seen which is the promise. When we have not received the promise or thing not seen, our faith stands in as the substance, but faith is not the thing not seen. If faith is not seen, then it would not stand trial. It may be intangible to us in the physical realm, but it is very real in the spirit realm. It is the substance, the actual existence of the things we are hoping for. If you are believing God for healing, healing becomes the thing not seen (the promise), It is not the evidence.

I had conditioned myself to believe that when I receive whatever I am believing God for, that the promise becomes the evidence to show that I have faith.

But it is the opposite, faith is the evidence that you will receive what you are asking for. It is the currency that is accepted in the spirit realm, the thing not seen or the promise is the commodity that you purchase with your faith. Our dollar is not good there. Faith is our purchasing power; it is not the promise. Increasing our purchasing power increases our wealth. We tend to put more work into acquiring the promise or thing not seen, instead of building or increasing our faith – our purchasing power.

For instance, while believing for the house, you my conduct research – market analysis, talk to real estate agents, tour couple homes, save for the downpayment, pray and pray. If after putting all these efforts to acquire the promise and it does not happen for you or come to fruition in your time frame, you may get offended and upset at God like the seed that fell on a rocky place. You feel like the time you put in believing for the promise was wasted. But that should not be the case. I have noticed that when I make it a priority to build my faith, apply my faith and I still do not receive the promise, I am not fazed. The time spent building my evidence is not wasted, because now my evidence has grown stronger and ready to continue to believe God for His will to be done here on earth as it is in heaven. If according to Hebrews 11:6 that it is impossible to please God without faith, then the time I put in building my faith and believing for the promise was not wasted, it was used in pleasing God so I can rejoice. This statement reflects the sentiments expressed by Habakkuk in chapter 3, verses 17-18 (TLB).

> [17] Even though the fig trees are all destroyed, and there is neither blossom left nor fruit; though the olive crops all fail, and the fields lie barren; even if the flocks die in the fields and the cattle barns are empty, [18] yet I will rejoice in the Lord; I will be happy in the God of my salvation.

By faith we believe that God exists, so it makes sense to approach Him by faith when believing for any of His promises. How do we make our request known to God by faith? I am a woman of a particular age child who has been declared infertile by medical science on account of diminishing ovarian egg reserve, age, early menopause, and past unsuccessful fertility treatments that is believing God for a baby. Before approaching the court of heaven with my petition, like any court of law I will need evidence to prove my case.

Step 1 – Gather the evidence (faith)

[17] So then faith comes by hearing, and hearing by the word of God.
Romans 10:17 (NKJV)

To obtain evidence, I find and study scriptures that support the "thing not seen" or the promise—in this case, the child I am believing God for. By "evidence," I mean scriptural passages or examples that give me confidence in what I am hoping for, even though I cannot see it yet. I look for precedent, knowing that if God fulfilled promises in the past, He can still do so now, because He is the same yesterday, today, and forever. With this foundation, I then present the following evidence to God:

➢ *Age is nothing but a number:*

"[13] Those that be planted in the house of the Lord shall flourish in the courts of our God. They shall still bring forth fruit in old age; they shall be fat and flourishing."
Psalm 92:13-14 (KJV)

Nub is the Hebrew word for fruit, and it means to increase, to germinate (to cause something to grow and develop).

Dasen is the Hebrew word for fat, and it means rich, fertile (able to conceive young)

So, I can boldly say that "at my age I am fruitful, I am fertile, I am able to conceive and thrive while doing it (flourishing)."

⁵ My soul [my life, my very self] is <u>satisfied</u> as with
marrow and <u>fatness</u>,
And my mouth offers praises [to You] with joyful lips.
Psalm 63:5 (AMP)

Saba is the Hebrew word for satisfy – to have enough, have plenty enough, to be sated. To be sated is to supply (someone) with as much as or more of something than is desired or can be managed.

Desen is the Hebrew word for fatness meaning abundance, luxuriance, fertility.

If you are a woman who has been called infertile, whose report will you believe? God satisfies you to the full with the ability to conceive.

> ➤ **Precedents:**

God gave Sarah a child in her old age in the Old Testament – Genesis 17:16-17 (NIV)

¹⁶ I will bless her and will surely give you a son by her. I will bless her so that she will be the mother of nations; kings of peoples will come from her." ¹⁷ Abraham fell facedown; he laughed and said to himself, "Will a son be born to a man a hundred years old? Will Sarah bear a child at the age of ninety?"

God also gave a child to righteous barren Elizabeth in her old age in the New Testament – Luke 1:6-7 (NIV)

⁶ Both of them were righteous in the sight of God, observing all the Lord's commands and decrees blamelessly. ⁷ But they were childless because Elizabeth was not able to conceive, and they were both very old.

The above scriptures gave me the precedent I needed to continue to present my case before God.

➤ **How will my petition glorify God?**

¹⁵ᵇ Has not the one God made you? You belong to him in body and spirit. And what does the one God seek? Godly offspring.
Malachi 2:15b (NIV)

¹⁹ For I have known (chosen, acknowledged) him [as My own], so that he may teach and command his children and [the sons of] his household after him to keep the way of the LORD by doing what is righteous and just, so that the LORD may bring upon Abraham what He has promised him."
Genesis 18:19 (AMP)

According to these scriptures, God desires godly offspring. He wants godly offsprings, I want a baby. It's a win-win situation. Therefore, I commit to raising my children in a manner that encourages them to develop a deep love and respect for Him.

➤ **God can do the impossible:**

God can close and open the womb like He did in the case of Hannah – 1 Samuel 1:5 & 20 (NIV)

⁵ But to Hannah he gave a double portion because he loved her, and the LORD had closed her womb.

²⁰ So in the course of time Hannah became pregnant and gave birth to a son. She named him Samuel, saying, "Because I asked the LORD for him."

➢ **Only God can give children:**

"Unless the Lord builds a house, the builders' work is useless."
Psalm 127:1b (TLB)

Bana is the Hebrew word for build, one of its meanings is to obtain children.

➢ *God is a rewarder of those who diligently seek Him.*

⁶ But without faith it is impossible to please Him, for he who comes to God must believe that He is, and that He is a rewarder of those who diligently seek Him.
Hebrews 11:6 (NKJV)

Misthapodotes is the Greek word for rewarder, and it means one who pays wages. One of the ways God pays wages when we seek Him diligently (crave, enquire, require) is by rewarding us with children.

³Children are a gift from God; they are his <u>reward</u>.
Psalm 127:3 (TLB)

Sakar – the Hebrew word for reward means wages, payment of contract, compensation, benefit. God gives benefits for worshipping him as seen in the following scriptures:

²⁵ You shall serve [only] the LORD your God, and He shall bless your bread and water. I will also remove sickness from among you. ²⁶ No one shall suffer miscarriage or be barren in your land; I will fulfill the number of your days.
Exodus 23:25-26 (AMP)

Blessed be the Lord, Who daily loads us with benefits, The God of our salvation! Selah
Psalm 68:19 (NKJV)

Bless the Lord, O my soul, And forget not all His benefits (rewards, recompense)
Psalm 103:2 (NKJV)

Children are one of the benefits we receive from the Lord our God.

Step 2 – Present your evidence and believe it.

Once I have compiled my evidence (God's word), the next step I take is what I call the thanksgiving walk. I enter His gates with thanksgiving and His court with praise, I then bring my petition to him with evidence from His word.

21 "Present your case," says the LORD.
"Set forth your arguments," says Jacob's King.
Isaiah 41:21(NIV)

Present is the Hebrew word **qarab** meaning to draw near, to enter into, to approach. The LORD – Jehovah (the existing one) is asking to us to approach Him with our case (cause, dispute, contention, adversary) and to bring forward our strong argument.

An attorney will refrain from presenting evidence that they do not believe will exonerate their client. The admissibility of his evidence in court will depend on its relevance and reliability. When he presents his evidence in court, it is subject to scrutiny by the opposing party. The judge issues a ruling grounded in the facts of the case, applicable laws, precedents, and presented evidence, rather than personal emotions.

Present your case before God like a lawyer in a courtroom. Remind Him of His word. I present the above evidence that I have gathered before God in prayer. Now that I have His attention, I am confident He will listen, as the evidence found in His word affirms:

12 The LORD said to me, "You have seen correctly, for I am watching to see that my word is fulfilled."
Jeremiah 1:12 (NIV)

Saqad is the Hebrew word for watching – to be wakeful over, to be alert i.e. sleepless, hence, to be on the lookout. We already know God does not slumber nor sleep, now we know why. He is on the lookout to make sure His word is fulfilled.

[11] so is my word that goes out from my mouth: It will not return to me empty,
but will accomplish what I desire and achieve the purpose for which I sent it.
Isaiah 55:11 (NIV)

Our job is to use the evidence to believe God for the things not seen (His promises), God watches His word to perform it (execute it, work it, perform it). We cannot make His word come to pass, He fulfils His word at His appointed time, but we can strengthen our believe in an infallible God.

[9] The Lord is not slow in keeping his promise, as some understand slowness. Instead he is patient with you, not wanting anyone to perish, but everyone to come to repentance.
2 Peter 3:9 (NIV)

God does not delay in keeping His promise as we understand delay. Our perception of slowness is different from God's. Remember Jonah, he gave the word to Nineveh and then waited to watch God rain down fire and brimstone on Nineveh. When that did not happen, he got angry with God for showing Nineveh mercy. God's ways and thoughts are higher than ours.

Step 3 – Trial of the evidence/faith.

After presenting your evidence, persecution will come to shake your faith to see if you believe your own evidence. In a natural court room, this is when the opposing lawyer will cross-examine you, challenge the evidence you presented and try to pick holes in it to shake its validity, to convince the judge and the jury to either throw the evidence out or to disbelieve it.

> ⁷ *That the trial of your faith, being much more precious than of gold that perisheth, though it be tried with fire, might be found unto praise and honour and glory at the appearing of Jesus Christ:*
> **1 Peter 1:7 (KJV)**

Gold is purified by fire to remove impurities. When gold is exposed to intense heat, impurities such as silver and copper rise to the surface and are removed, leaving behind pure gold. In a similar way, our faith is tested through life's challenges to prove its genuineness and trustworthiness. Just as gold endures intense heat to become pure, our faith may go through difficult trials that refine and strengthen our trust in God. When our faith is tried and stands the test, it brings praise, glory, and honor to our Lord, Jesus Christ.

When our faith is tested, the worries, doubts, unbelief, and selfishness mixed in with our faith often rise to the surface. In these moments, we are given the opportunity to confess our unbelief, let go of doubt and worry, and allow genuine faith to shine through.

When trouble or persecution arises because of the word— because of your faith, the "evidence" that you hold onto—will you continue to trust God? If you finally become pregnant without intervention after being told it was impossible and then face the heartbreak of a miscarriage, will you still trust God? If you go through multiple failed egg retrievals and are told you're no longer a candidate for treatment, will you continue to believe? Will you cling to your evidence, or will despair take over? Remember and take courage that at 90 years old Sarah's eggs must have turned to ashes, yet the impossible became possible.

Strengthen your faith, strengthen your evidence. In a courtroom, if someone's evidence is weak, they may simply hope the judge will acquit them out of mercy. Similarly, our heavenly Father shows mercy to whomever He chooses. Exodus 2:24 tells of the Israelites groaning in slavery and crying out for help; God heard their cry and sent a deliverer. This shows that God responds to sincere cries for help, reinforcing the importance of both faith and seeking mercy. In Mark 9 when Jesus healed the boy possessed by an evil Spirit, Jesus told the boy's father that everything is possible to the one who believes. This illustrates that faith opens the door to God's power and mercy, highlighting the necessity of belief in experiencing divine intervention.

[21] Jesus asked the boy's father, "How long has he been like this?" "From childhood," he answered. [22] "It has often thrown him into fire or water to kill him. But if you <u>can</u> do anything, take pity on us and help us." [23] "'If you <u>can</u>'?" said Jesus. "<u>Everything is possible for one who believes.</u>" [24] Immediately the boy's father exclaimed, "<u>I do believe</u>; help me overcome my <u>unbelief!</u>"
Mark 9:21-24 (NIV)

Pisteuo is the Greek word for believe meaning to have faith. Jesus is saying here that anything is possible to the one who has faith. The boy's father responded, "I do have faith, help me overcome my unbelief." The boy's father acknowledged his weak faith and asked for help. Jesus rebuked the unclean spirit and the boy was healed. God's mercies are new every morning and is available in our moment of weakness. Ultimately, while faith and evidence are important, God's mercy is what completes the process when our faith is weak and any opportunity to believe God for his promises is a chance to strengthen our faith in Him.

Step 4 – Wait.

If a desire is deep within you, don't give up on it. Believe your evidence during the waiting season. There is a waiting time between the presentation of the evidence and the manifestation of the promise. In a court of law, the judge typically allocates sufficient time to thoroughly deliberate the case, examine the presented evidence, consider relevant precedents, and apply the appropriate legal principles. We sometimes want to throw in the towel at this stage, thinking maybe it is not God's will, and then switch to plan B.

Elijah did not stop praying until the seventh time when his servant saw a small cloud the size of a human fist. You may say but that's a really small cloud, yet it bolstered his faith, the small cloud was the sign he needed that He has received the answer to his prayer. The posture of prayer was Elijah's one and only plan.

⁶I have set watchmen upon thy walls, O Jerusalem, which shall never hold their peace day nor night: ye that make mention of the LORD, keep not silence, ⁷And give him no rest, till he establish, and till he make Jerusalem a praise in the earth.
Isaiah 62:6-7 (NIV)

Persistently seek God while you wait. To rest is to be quiet, to be silent, to cease, to pause. All the things we are told not to do while we are petitioning God. To keep silent is to be inactive. Waiting is not a time of inactivity. It is the time of speaking – you could be confessing the word, meditating on the word, praising God, engaging in thanksgiving. The waiting is a time of productive engagement and preparation because we know that He who promised is faithful.

6 And the Lord said, "Listen to what the unjust judge says. 7 And will not God bring about justice for his chosen ones, who cry out to him day and night? Will he keep putting them off? 8 I tell you, he will see that they get justice, and quickly. However, when the Son of Man comes, will he find faith on the earth?"
Luke 18: 6-8 (NIV)

You have made your closing argument, do not get weary in well doing because the judge of all men is on your side.

Why is our faith tested?

1. To bring praise and honor to God

I am reminded of the three Hebrew boys – Shadrach, Meshach and Abednego. When King Nebuchadnezzar told them to bow to his golden image or be thrown into the fiery furnace. They replied,

¹⁶ Shadrach, Meshach, and Abednego, answered and said to the king, O Nebuchadnezzar, we are not careful to answer thee in this matter. ¹⁷ If it be so, our God whom we serve is able to deliver us from the burning fiery furnace, and he will deliver us out of thine hand, O king. ¹⁸ But if not, be it known unto thee, O king, that we will not serve thy gods, nor worship the golden image which thou hast set up.
Daniel 3:16-18 (NIV)

It was not even a topic worth thinking over, they told the King. These men were willing to die rather than bow their knees to another god. I think they must have read Isaiah 43:2-4 because we know from scripture that God gave them knowledge and skill in all kinds of literature (they were well read and educated), Daniel is noted to have read the book of Jeremiah to understand when the captivity of Jerusalem would end.

When you walk through the fire, you will not be burned; the flames will not set you ablaze. ³ For I am the Lord your God, the Holy One of Israel, your Savior; I give Egypt for your ransom,
Cush and Seba in your stead. ⁴ Since you are precious and honored in my sight,
and because I love you, I will give people in exchange for you,
nations in exchange for your life. Isaiah 43:2-4 (NIV)

Their faith – the evidence of things not seen was the word they knew, and it rested in the God they served. God true to His word gave men in exchange for these three men because the flame of the fire killed the men who carried them in. We all have had our share of trials and tribulations, but I think I would be right to say that in our part of the world the opportunity to die physically for our faith has never presented itself like it did for these gentlemen. Their faith in God was literally tested by fire.

[28] *Then Nebuchadnezzar said, "Praise be to the God of Shadrach, Meshach and Abednego, who has sent his angel and rescued his servants! They trusted in him and defied the king's command and were willing to give up their lives rather than serve or worship any god except their own God.* [29] *Therefore I decree that the people of any nation or language who say anything against the God of Shadrach, Meshach and Abednego be cut into pieces and their houses be turned into piles of rubble, for no other god can save in this way."*

[30] *Then the king promoted Shadrach, Meshach and Abednego in the province of Babylon.*
Daniel 3: 28-30 (NIV)

The trial of their faith brought praise and honor to God. King Nebuchadnezzar commended and promoted them for their wiliness to give up their lives for their God. This must have been the time when the seed of the gospel was sown in the heart of King Nebuchadnezzar, it created an awareness of the presence and power of the Most High God. We see him later in chapter 4, a pagan king praising and applauding the miracles of God.

King Nebuchadnezzar, To the nations and peoples of every language, who live in all the earth: May you prosper greatly! ²It is my pleasure to tell you about the miraculous signs and wonders that the Most High God has performed for me. ³How great are his signs, how mighty his wonders! His kingdom is an eternal kingdom; his dominion endures from generation to generation.
Daniel 4:1-3 (NIV)

Also, after Kind Nebuchadnezzar lost his mind for 7 years as punishment from God for his pride, at the end of the 7 years, he praised God and regained his mind.

2. To produce patience

²My brethren, count it all joy when you fall into various trials, ³knowing that the testing of your faith produces patience. ⁴ But let patience have its perfect work, that you may be perfect and complete, lacking nothing.
James 1:2-4 (NKJV)

When our faith is tested it produces patience. The Greek word **hypomone** – meaning endurance, perseverance. Patience is the capacity to accept or tolerate delay, trouble, or suffering without getting angry or upset.

Who do we become when the "thing not seen" or the promise is delayed or even denied? Do we become disenchanted, and throw in the towel or do we push on?

[18] *Against all hope, Abraham in hope believed and so became the father of many nations, just as it had been said to him, "So shall your offspring be."[[19] Without weakening in his <u>faith,</u> he faced the fact that his body was as good as dead—since he was about a hundred years old—and that Sarah's womb was also dead. [20] Yet he did not waver through unbelief regarding the <u>promise of God,</u> but was strengthened in his faith and gave glory to God, [21] being fully persuaded that God had power to do what he had promised. [22] This is why "it was credited to him as righteousness."*
Romans 4:18-22 (NIV)

Have you ever believed against all hope? My old way of thinking would have assumed that Abraham received evidence of his faith when he had Isaac. But that is far from the truth. His evidence/faith remained strong even when he did not see the promise, he did not waver in his faith. I do not think this was an easy feat for Abraham and Sarah. The promise of a child was made to him by God when he was 75 years old, Isaac was born when he was 100 years old. For 25 years against all hope he believed, his faith never weakened because his faith rested in the God who made the promise.

What amazes me is how he separated his Faith from the facts. His faith rested in the creator of life, but he faced the fact that his body was dead, and his wife was past childbearing age. He did not deny that fact. God had told him to leave his people, his family, his land and go to another land that He will show him, a land where he will make him a great nation (Genesis 12: 1-3). Abraham obeyed God, left the known for the unknown and yet for 25 years he never turned back or said:

"Sarah, I must have heard God wrong, it's been 25 years now and we have not seen this promise of a child, talk less of a great nation, let's pack up and head home?"

- No, they persevered.

Sarah honored the word of God that He spoke through Abraham even though:

> **Abraham had resigned himself to the idea that his servant would inherit his estate-**

After this, the word of the LORD came to Abram in a vision:"Do not be afraid, Abram.
I am your shield, your very great reward."[2] But Abram said, "Sovereign LORD, what can you give me since I remain childless and the one who will inherit my estate is Eliezer of Damascus?"[3] And Abram said, "You have given me no children; so a servant in

my household will be my heir."[4] Then the word of the LORD came to him: "This man will not be your heir, but a son who is

your own flesh and blood will be your heir."
Genesis 15: 1-4 (NIV)

➢ **They had a moment of trying to help God along:**

Now Sarai, Abram's wife, had borne him no children. But she had an Egyptian slave named Hagar; ²so she said to Abram, "The LORD has kept me from having children. Go, sleep with my slave; perhaps I can build a family through her." Abram agreed to what Sarai said.
Genesis 16:1-2 (NIV)

➢ **At some point Abraham tried to bargain with God to make Ishmael the child of promise:**

¹⁷Abraham fell facedown; he laughed and said to himself, "Will a son be born to a man a hundred years old? Will Sarah bear a child at the age of ninety?" ¹⁸And Abraham said to God, "If only Ishmael might live under your blessing!" ¹⁹Then God said, "Yes, but your wife Sarah will bear you a son, and you will call him Isaac. I will establish my covenant with him as an everlasting covenant for his descendants after him.
Genesis 17: 17-19 (NIV)

➢ **Sarah laughed at God's promise:**

[13] Then the Lord said to Abraham, "Why did Sarah laugh and say, 'How can I give birth to a child when I am so old?' [14] Is anything too hard for the Lord? I will return to you at this time next year, and Sarah will have a son."
Genesis 18: 13-14 (NIV)

Abraham and Sarah's faith were proved for 25 years and for 25 years they remained steadfast, unwavering. They believed God would fulfil his word. They did not give God a deadline. Their trust in God did not waiver though the promise was delayed, their faith remained.

21 Now the LORD was gracious to Sarah as he had said, and the LORD did for Sarah what he had promised. [2] Sarah became pregnant and bore a son to Abraham in his old age, at the very time God had promised him. [6] Sarah said, "God has brought me laughter, and everyone who hears about this will laugh with me." [7] And she added, "Who would have said to Abraham that Sarah would nurse children? Yet I have borne him a son in his old age."
Genesis 21:1-2 & 6-7 (NIV)

Abraham persevered and God fulfilled the promise to Abraham at the very time He had promised him.

♦ *Separate your faith from the fact and use every trial as an opportunity to strengthen your faith.*

3. That we may please God.

6 But without faith it is impossible to [walk with God and] please Him, for whoever comes [near] to God must [necessarily] believe that God exists and that He rewards those who [earnestly and diligently] seek Him.
Hebrews 11:6 AMP

To please someone is to make them happy or to give them pleasure. When we exercise our faith by standing on God's word to see His promise fulfilled in our lives, it pleases Him. Because we are by faith declaring that He exists and He rewards our act of faith.

After Abraham received the promised Isaac, his faith was tested. He had waited 25 years for the promise of a son, then in Genesis God spoke to him:

1 Now after these things, God tested [the faith and commitment of] Abraham and said to him, "Abraham!" And he answered, "Here I am." 2 God said, "Take now your son, your only son [of promise], whom you love, Isaac, and go to the region of Moriah, and offer him there as a burnt offering on one of the mountains of which I shall tell you." 3 So Abraham got up early in the morning, saddled his donkey, and took two of his young men with him and his son Isaac; and he split the wood for the burnt offering, and then he got up and went to the place of which God had told him.
Genesis 22:1-3 (AMP)

Hold up, how did we get here? If I heard that, I will say the devil is a liar, no way will God tell me to sacrifice my child, my only child. This verse is often read without considering that Abraham's obedience may have required significant personal effort, tears and heartache. Abraham not only said yes, but he did it early in the morning. His obedience was swift. He made preparation for the sacrifice - he split the wood for the offering, carried a fire and a knife. He didn't suggest waiting on God, fasting, praying about the decision, or questioning if he heard correctly.

As I ponder Abraham's experience, I can't help but wonder— did he question whether the God he had faithfully walked with for more than twenty years would ever ask him to do something so contrary to His loving nature? I wonder what was going through Abraham's mind as he prepared for that journey to Moriah? Did Abraham share this information with Sarah, or did he keep the depth of God's command to himself, telling her only that he and Isaac were going to make a sacrifice to the Lord? If Abraham had told Sarah, how did that conversation go? How did he break the news to her? Maybe, in a hushed, steady voice, he told her, "Mother of many nations, God has asked me to take our son, our only son, to the mountain and offer him as a sacrifice."

How did Sarah respond? Did she nod and say, "Yes, my lord, as the Lord wills"? Did the breaking of that news break her? Did she collapse in tears on the floor? I imagine the weight of obedience was heavy between Sarah and Abraham that day.

When I think of this moment, I am filled with questions I long to ask Sarah one day in eternity. Did she kiss her son goodbye trusting that she would see her son again, clinging to the promises spoken over their family? Or did she spend the day anxiously praying, wrestling with the unknown? How did Abraham find the strength to walk in obedience, and what emotions swirled beneath his outward composure? How do we respond when faith challenges us in ways that seem to contradict everything we understand about God's character?

This is what pleasing faith is about, it is a total unquestionable trust in God – all of God, His nature, His love, His power, His goodness. A faith that rests solely on God's word, not on the promise.

In the beginning [before all time] was the Word (Christ), and the Word was with God, and the Word was God Himself. ² He was [continually existing] in the beginning [co-eternally] with God.
John 1:1-2 (AMP)

If our faith rests unconditionally on His Word which is Him, then the promise or benefits follows us automatically as we walk with Him. Why? Because He rewards those who diligently/earnestly seek Him. His goodness and his mercy follow us as we follow Him.

Surely goodness and mercy and unfailing love shall follow me all the days of my life,
And I shall dwell forever [throughout all my days] in the house and in the presence of the Lord.
Psalm 23:6

Abraham's faith was deeply rooted in his ongoing relationship with God. During his 25-year period of anticipating a son, he cultivated a relationship with God marked by repeated consistent acts of obedience, meaningful encounters and exceeding compensations from God. For instance, when God called Abraham to leave his homeland and journey to an unknown land (Genesis 12), Abraham responded without hesitation, demonstrating his trust and willingness to follow God's direction. Throughout the years, Abraham's obedience was evident in moments such as building altars to the Lord and making an everlasting covenant between God, Abraham and his descendants. Circumcision was the sign of that covenant. Based on that legally binding agreement God promises to bless him, to give him an heir, to make his descendants numerous (Genesis 12:7–8; 13:18). Abraham showed compassionate engagement with God's purposes by faithfully interceding for the people of Sodom (Genesis 18:22–33).

Abraham's relationship with God was not distant or formal; rather, it was intimate and personal. For example, in Genesis 18, God visits Abraham, wines and dines with him, symbolizing their close fellowship and mutual respect. This unique bond is further affirmed in Isaiah 41:8, where Abraham is referred to as God's friend, highlighting the depth of trust and affection between them. By the time God commanded Abraham to sacrifice Isaac he was already familiar with God's voice, he knew God's modus operandi. It was not a demand made to a stranger, but to someone who had consistently walked with God, witnessed His faithfulness, and developed a profound sense of loyalty and reliance on Him.

Abraham's journey with God—characterized by dialogue, obedience, and shared experiences—shaped a faith that could withstand even the most challenging tests, making his story both engaging and insightful for us who are seeking to understand the nature of pleasing faith. So, Abraham based on the evidence of things not seen, obeyed God and took his one and only son, his promise from God to sacrifice.

> *[19] Abraham reasoned that God could even raise the dead, and so in a manner of speaking he did receive Isaac back from death.*
> **Hebrews 11:19 (NIV)**

Our faith, though as small as a mustard seed that can move mountains will be tested. When I receive the promise of a child, that will not be my evidence. I am simply building my faith, which is and remains the evidence.

> *[13] All these people were still living by faith when they died. **They did not receive the things promised**; they only saw them and welcomed them from a distance, admitting that they were foreigners and strangers on earth. [14] People who say such things show that they are looking for a country of their own. [15] If they had been thinking of the country they had left, they would have had opportunity to return. [16] Instead, they were longing for a better country—a heavenly one. Therefore God is not ashamed to be called their God, for he has prepared a city for them.*
> **Hebrews 11:13 (NIV)**

*[33] Who through faith subdued kingdoms, wrought righteousness, **obtained promises,** stopped the mouths of lions. [39] These were all commended for their faith, yet none of them received what had been promised, [40] since God had planned something better for us so that only together with us would they be made perfect.*
Hebrews 11:33 &39-40 (NIV)

In verse 33 – one group received the promise/things not seen through FAITH while in verse 13 and 39 another group did not receive the promise/things not seen through FAITH and yet both groups were commended for their faith. That tells me that the promise or things not seen are temporary but the evidence - our faith is eternal, we receive commendation for having faith in God. Jesus said in Matthew 6:19-21(NIV)

[19] "Do not store up for yourselves treasures on earth, where moths and vermin destroy, and where thieves break in and steal. [20] But store up for yourselves treasures in heaven, where moths and vermin do not destroy, and where thieves do not break in and steal. [21] For where your treasure is, there your heart will be also.

There have been instances where individuals believed that they would be healed of life-threatening illnesses yet ultimately passed away without experiencing the anticipated recovery. Did they not have faith? Of course they did, their faith in God is the evidence. Did they receive the promise of healing? Yes, but not on this earth. They went to a place without sickness. God is not ashamed to be called their God because their faith pleased Him. This tells me that:

- *Our victory does not only come in the form of earthly conquests.*

We are sojourners on earth so limiting our victory to earth alone is short-sighted. Paul captured it best in Philippians 1:21(AMP):

> *21 For to me, to live is Christ [He is my source of joy, my reason to live] and to die is gain [for I will be with Him in eternity].*

Also, in1 Corinthians 15:19 (NKJV)

> *19 If in this life only we have hope in Christ, we are of all men most miserable.*

With this mindset we can live purposefully and intentionally. If we treasure our faith which is more precious than gold that perishes, we will not lose faith or deny Christ when we do not receive the promise, or the things not seen on this earth. We can say like the Hebrew boys, "whether God saves us from the fire or through the fire, we will not bow our knee to another God." Another God can be money, fame, fruit of the womb, wealth, beauty, politics etc.

Our faith (the evidence) is more valuable than the thing not seen (the promise), if we grasp that understanding it will change how we walk with God and how we wait on God. We will wait with the goal of refining and building our faith to please him along with the expectation of receiving the thing not seen.

CHAPTER FOUR

THE SEASON OF CORRECTION IN RIGHTEOUSNESS

*"All scripture is given by inspiration of God, and is profitable for doctrine, for reproof, for **correction,** for instruction in righteousness: [17] That the man of God may be perfect, thoroughly furnished unto all good works.*

2 Timothy 3:16-17

The Greek word for correction is **epanorthosis**, which means restoration to an upright or a right state, improvement of life or character, straightening up again (often after acting badly), rectification (to put something right), restoration (to return back to its original condition).

Restoring an individual to an upright status indicates that they have, at some point, forfeited or lost their prior standing. Sin carries a heavy weight and can slow down our walk with God causing us to miss the promises and move of God as we go from season to season. Hebrews 12:1 tells us to lay aside the heavy weight and the sin that entangles us so that we can run with perseverance the race marked out for us. This weight of sin can either drive us further away from God or in humility drive us to our knees to God.

⁴ My guilt has overwhelmed me like a burden too heavy to bear. ⁵ My wounds fester and are loathsome because of my sinful folly. ⁶ <u>I am bowed down and brought very low</u>; all day long I go about mourning. ²¹ Lord, do not forsake me; do not be far from me, my God.
²² Come quickly to help me, my Lord and my Savior.
Psalm 38:4-6,21-22 (NIV)

To be brought low is to humble oneself before God in repentance. It is to acknowledge and confront one's errors with a contrite heart The word of God can straighten us up again, it can bring us back in alignment with God, set us back on the right course if we repent after sinning. This chapter examines the experiences of David, Job, Peter, Paul, and the Samaritan woman—five individuals who underwent restoration to an upright state.

> ➤ **David**

David said in Psalm 119:11:

¹¹ I have hidden your word in my heart that I might not sin against you.

David is an example of someone who made significant errors and sought **epanorthosis** (restoration). From his experience he writes that to live sin free we must hide/store the word of God in our hearts.

During a time when it was customary for kings to participate in warfare, the scripture says David remained at home (2 Samuel 11:1). David became involved in a relationship with Bathsheba, the wife of one of his soldiers, Uriah. As a result of this adulterous affair, David fathered a child. In an effort to conceal his actions, he manipulated Uriah, trying to get him drunk enough to sleep with his wife so he could pin the child on him. When this plan failed, David ultimately arranged for Uriah's death to conceal his sin. To kill Uriah, he ordered his army commander to deviate from conventional warfare protocols by fighting near the city wall and placing Uriah where enemy archers could easily strike him. This scheme led not only to Uriah's death, but also to the loss of several of David's servants. David's choice to conceal his wrongdoing set off a series of avoidable mistakes, illustrating the destructive consequences of trying to cover up wrongdoing instead of facing it directly.

When Nathan the prophet confronted David with the truth, David was forced to see himself reflected in the mirror of God's word. Nathan's words forced David to confront the gravity of his actions, leading to genuine remorse and a turning point in his life. Deeply moved and convicted, David immediately repented, acknowledging both his guilt and need for restoration.

[13] Then David said to Nathan, "I have sinned against the LORD." Nathan replied, "The LORD has taken away your sin. You are not going to die. [14] But because by doing this you have shown utter contempt for the LORD, the son born to you will die."
2 Samuel 12:13 (NIV)

Out of David's brokenness and acknowledgment of his transgression came the beautiful Psalm 51 (AMP) – a passionate prayer of forgiveness where he renounced his sin:

Have mercy on me, O God, according to Your lovingkindness;
According to the greatness of Your compassion blot out my transgressions.
2 Wash me thoroughly from my wickedness and guilt
And cleanse me from my sin.
3 For I am conscious of my transgressions and I acknowledge them;
My sin is always before me.

He traced the root of his sin to the womb: what we don't confront we cannot correct.

5 I was brought forth in [a state of] wickedness;
In sin my mother conceived me [and from my beginning I, too, was sinful].

He asked God to restore him:

10 Create in me a clean heart, O God, And renew a right and steadfast spirit within me.
11 Do not cast me away from Your presence And do not take Your Holy Spirit from me.
12 Restore to me the joy of Your salvation And sustain me with a willing spirit.

Finally, he pledged to guide those who have gone astray toward a relationship with God:

> ¹³ *Then I will teach transgressors Your ways, And sinners shall be converted and return to You.*

We know that David and Bathsheba went on to have another child:

> *She gave birth to a son, and they named him Solomon. The LORD loved him; ²⁵ and because the LORD loved him, he sent word through Nathan the prophet to name him Jedidiah.*
> **2 Samuel 12:24b-25 (NIV)**

The purpose of the inspired word of God is to restore us to an upright position when we have fallen short of God's glory. Through His word God made room, provision for our humanity. We do not have to beat ourselves up when we fall and stay down. That is what the enemy wants. If we stay down, our enemy gets the victory.

> ➤ *Peter*

What about when Satan makes a demand to sift us like wheat as was the case for Peter?

> ³¹ *And the Lord said, Simon, Simon, behold, Satan hath desired to have you, that he may sift you as wheat: ³² But I have prayed for thee, that thy faith fail not: and when thou art*

converted, strengthen thy brethren. ³³And he said unto him, Lord, I am ready to go with thee, both into prison, and to death.
Luke 22: 31-33 (AMP)

Hath desired in Greek is **exaiteo** meaning to ask that one be given up to one from the power of another, in a bad sense for torture or for punishment, to demand, desire. Satan demanded permission to sift Peter.

Siniazo is the Greek word for to sift – an inward agitation to try one's faith to the verge of overthrow.

Picture this: the devil went to God and demanded permission to agitate and overthrow (defeat) Peter's faith. However, Jesus prayed that Peter's faith would not fail him. He also charged Peter to strengthen his brothers when he is restored to loving and obeying God—when he got back up, not if. Jesus's words remind us that failure is not final—Peter will rise again, and his renewed strength will help others.

⁶⁰But Peter said, "Man, I do not know what you are talking about." Immediately, while he was still speaking, a rooster crowed. ⁶¹The Lord turned and looked at Peter. And Peter remembered the word of the Lord, how He had told him, "Before a rooster crows today, you will deny Me three times."
Luke 22:60-61(NIV)

Peter fell into the sin of denying Jesus not once, but 3 times. When Jesus looked him, Peter saw mercy, he saw love, he saw his friend, his Lord and savior:

⁶² And he went out and wept bitterly [deeply grieved and distressed].
Luke 22:62 (NIV)

Peter's faith in Christ did not fail, he was able to get back up and strengthen his brothers. According to Acts chapter 2, his sermon on Pentecost resulted in approximately three thousand people joining the disciples that day. Peter's experience is both encouraging and inspiring, reinforcing the message of hope and resilience for all who stumble but choose to rise again.

> ➢ *Job*

Job is another example of the enemy going to God for permission to overthrow a believer's faith. Job is described as the greatest among the men of the east. He was wealthy: Job possessed seven thousand sheep, three thousand camels, five hundred yokes of oxen, five hundred female donkeys, and a very large household until one day:

⁶ One day the angels came to present themselves before the Lord, and Satan[b] also came with them. ⁷ The Lord said to Satan, "Where have you come from?" Satan answered the Lord, "From roaming throughout the earth, going back and forth on it."

⁸ Then the Lord said to Satan, "Have you considered my servant Job? There is no one on earth like him; he is blameless and upright, a man who fears God and shuns evil."

⁹ Then Satan answered the LORD and said, "Does Job fear God for no reason? ¹⁰ Have you not put a hedge around him and his house and all that he has, on every side? You have blessed the work of his hands, and his possessions have increased in the land. ¹¹ But stretch out your hand and touch all that he has, and he will curse you to your face." ¹² And the LORD said to Satan, "Behold, all that he has is in your hand. Only against him do not stretch out your hand." So Satan went out from the presence of the LORD.
Job 1:6-12 (NIV)

Job experienced the loss of all his property, the death of his seven children in a single day, and he was stricken with painful sores that covered his body from head to toe. I cannot imagine the grieve and brokenness of this man. His wife told him to curse God and die but he refused, He held onto faith while maintaining his righteousness.

²² In all this Job did not sin or charge God with wrong.
Job 1:22 (NJKV)

When God confronted Job for declaring that God had treated him unjustly, Job repented right away:

⁵ I had heard of you by the hearing of the ear, but now my eye sees you;
⁶ therefore I despise myself, and repent in dust and ashes."
Job 42:5-6 (NIV)

God gave Job the task of standing in the gap for his friends so that they would not face God's judgement for not speaking right about God.

⁷After the Lord had said these things to Job, he said to Eliphaz the Temanite, "I am angry with you and your two friends, because you have not spoken the truth about me, as my servant Job has. ⁸So now take seven bulls and seven rams and go to my servant Job and sacrifice a burnt offering for yourselves. My servant Job will pray for you, and I will accept his prayer and not deal with you according to your folly. You have not spoken the truth about me, as my servant Job has." ⁹So Eliphaz the Temanite, Bildad the Shuhite and Zophar the Naamathite did what the Lord told them; and the Lord accepted Job's prayer.
Job 42:7-9 (NIV)

God restores Job and blesses him with double for all his trouble after he prayed for his friends.

¹⁰After Job had prayed for his friends, the Lord restored his fortunes and gave him twice as much as he had before.
Job 42:10 (NIV)

> ➤ **Apostle Paul**

Another person of interest is Apostle Paul, formerly known as Saul. Prior to his conversion he had approved the death of Stephen.

⁵⁸ Then they drove him out of the city and began stoning him; and the witnesses placed their outer robes at the feet of a young man named Saul. ⁵⁹ They continued stoning Stephen as he called on the Lord and said, "Lord Jesus, receive and accept and welcome my spirit!" ⁶⁰ Then falling on his knees [in worship], he cried out loudly, "Lord, do not hold this sin against them [do not charge them]!" When he had said this, he fell asleep [in death].
Acts 7:58-60(APM)

8 Saul wholeheartedly approved of Stephen's death
Acts 8:1(AMP)

Saul was on his way to Damascus to persecute the followers of Christ when God encountered him. He had obtained approval from the high priest to find and arrest Christians. He was zealous for the Jewish faith, but God interrupted him and gave him one assignment: to proclaim Christ to both Jews and Gentiles. We see in Acts 9 and 10 how Saul's repentance and conversion were immediate. His road to repentance started by his awareness that he was a sinner that needed a savior. Saul erroneously thought he was doing the work of God, until our Lord confronted him with his sin.

⁴ and he fell to the ground and heard a voice [from heaven] saying to him, "Saul, Saul, why are you persecuting and oppressing Me?" ⁵ And Saul said, "Who are You, Lord?" And He answered, "I am Jesus whom you are persecuting, ⁶ now get up and go into the city, and you will be told what you must do." Acts 9:4-6 (AMP)

God sent Ananias to pray for Saul and to convert him to Christ.

> [17] So Ananias left and entered the house, and he laid his hands on Saul and said, "Brother Saul, the Lord Jesus, who appeared to you on the road as you came [to Damascus], has sent me so that you may regain your sight and be filled with the Holy Spirit [in order to proclaim Christ to both Jews and Gentiles]." [18] Immediately something like scales fell from Saul's eyes, and he regained his sight. Then he got up and was baptized; [19] and he took some food and was strengthened.
> **Acts 9:17-19 (AMP)**

After Paul's conversion, he immediately started preaching salvation to others.

> For several days [afterward] Saul remained with the disciples who were at Damascus. [20] And immediately he began proclaiming Jesus in the synagogues, saying, "This Man is the Son of God [the promised Messiah]!"
> **Acts 9:19-20 (AMP)**

> ➤ **The Samaritan Woman**

She was the parched soul at Jacob's well whose story is only mentioned in the book of John. She was the one that Jesus made a purposeful detour to Samaria, choosing to meet her at her brokenness.

His arrival was not accidental but for her that day was just like any other day. Yet this seemingly ordinary day was a divine intersection that was written before creation. It marked the day when a single heart's restoration would ignite salvation across a city.

Jesus did not perform any miracles to her or for her, He saw her. Jesus saw beyond the outward thirst for water to the inner drought that had driven her from one empty embrace to another. When He spoke to her, He spoke not only to her situation but to her soul. His words awakened the hope that had laid dormant in her heart for a while stirring a flood of conviction that brought repentance within her gentle heart.

The effect of Jesus's words was like rain falling on dry ground. She drank in His words, which became an overflowing well of living water within her. The effect of His words was immediate, she dropped everything and ran to proclaim the good news of salvation, "I have met my Messiah, the anointed one who told me everything I have ever done,"

[28] Then the woman left her water jar and went into the city and began telling the people, [29] "Come, see a man who told me all the things that I have done! Can this be the Christ (the Messiah, the Anointed)?" [30] So the people left the city and were coming to Him. [39] Now many Samaritans from that city believed in Him and trusted Him [as Savior] because of what the woman said when she testified, "He told me all the things that I have done.
John 4: 28-30&39 (AMP)

This was a come, see, change type of evangelism. For the people to believe in her account of what had transpired at the well, there must have been an undeniable transformation in her that stirred curiosity and faith among her neighbors drawing them out of their homes to come and see the messiah. Through her, we witness how a single moment of grace can spread like wildfire—bringing healing, hope, and transformation to all who were willing to come and see. They believed in Jesus, they came to Jesus, they saw Jesus, and they were changed by Jesus all due to the witness of one woman.

> [42] and they told the woman, "We no longer believe just because of what you said; for [now] we have heard Him for ourselves and know [with confident assurance] that this One is truly the Savior of [all] the world."
> **John 4: 42**

Upon observing these five individuals during their period of correction, it was evident that each underwent a similar progression: **repentance, restoration, and subsequently the proclamation of salvation to others.** They are the key attributes of genuine change. To judge true repentance, focus on actions, not emotions or statements, by their fruits you will know them (Matthew 7:20 NKJV).

David immediately repented when the prophet Nathan pointed out his sin to him, Peter wept bitterly when Jesus looked at him after he denied Him 3 times. Job repented in dust and ashes. Paul's repentance and baptism happened simultaneously. The Samaritan woman had an immediate recognition that she was standing before the prophesied messiah, His words brought immediate repentance and change.

¹⁰ Godly sorrow brings repentance that leads to salvation and leaves no regret, but worldly sorrow brings death.
2 Corinthians 7:10 (NIV)

All five individuals showed examples of godly sorrow bringing repentance that led to their restoration and salvation of others. David promises if restored that he would teach transgressors God's ways and convert sinners to return to God. Peter was charged by Jesus to strengthen and support his brothers [in the faith] when he is restored, his Pentecost sermon brought thousands to the Lord. Job prayed for his friends so that God would not deal with them according to their folly. Saul after being restored immediately started preaching Jesus. The Samaritan ran into her city and proclaimed the good news of salvation. Through her vulnerability and willingness to be used by God, salvation came and illuminated Samaria with the light of redemption.

♦ *This is the true purpose of the season of correction – to raise us up, to straighten us, to restore us so we can point men to Christ.*

¹⁵ For we are the sweet fragrance of Christ [which ascends] to God, [discernible both] among those who are being saved and among those who are perishing; ¹⁶ to the latter one an aroma from death to death [a fatal, offensive odor], but to the

other an aroma from life to life [a vital fragrance, living and
fresh]
2 Corinthians 2:15-17 (AMP)

Out of our brokenness must come a sweet fragrance drawing
men to the savior and to salvation.

¹⁶ For a righteous man falls seven times, and rises again,
But the wicked stumble in time of disaster and collapse.
Proverbs 24:16 (AMP)

Proverbs 24:16 scripture is not a license to continue to sin. It
is important to differentiate between falling into sin and
walking in sin. Falling into sin refers to a momentary lapse or
mistake, while walking in sin describes a continuous lifestyle
of sin. Understanding this difference is crucial for spiritual
growth. When a righteous person falls, they feel sorrowful,
repent, accept God's restorative work and then humbly
points others to the savior. They appropriate the precious
blood of Jesus for forgiveness and cleansing.

Walking in sin is a habitual pattern. The habitual sinner takes
God's grace for granted, wallows in sin believing that God
would forgive him anyway as long he asks for forgiveness,
showing a pattern of disregard for God's guidance.

What shall we say [to all this]? Should we continue in sin and
practice sin as a habit so that [God's gift of] grace may
increase and overflow? ² Certainly not! How can we, the very

ones who died to sin, continue to live in it any longer?
Romans 6:1-2 (AMP)

Walking in sin means making a consistent habit of choosing actions and attitudes that go against the word of God, rather than occasionally making mistakes and seeking true repentance and forgiveness. This kind of pattern often signals that a stronghold is at play in someone's life. A stronghold is a deeply rooted way of thinking or behaving that keeps a person from experiencing true spiritual freedom— it's spiritually fortified mental or emotional fortress influences decisions and holds people back from understanding and appropriating the power of the cross and living in the light of what Christ accomplished. For example, if someone often struggles with lust and finds it controlling their reactions, that lust could be a stronghold. The stronghold will have to be demolished for sin to loosen its grip.

[4] The weapons we fight with are not the weapons of the world. On the contrary, they have divine power to demolish strongholds.
2 Corinthians 10:4 (NIV)

Overcoming a stronghold starts with recognizing its presence and then using the power of the cross, which means relying on Jesus' victory over sin and seeking His help to change. We demolish strongholds with the mighty weapons God has given us – fasting and prayer, the word of God, the blood of Jesus, the belt of truth, the shield of faith, the helmet of salvation, the breastplate of righteousness and feet that is fitted with the gospel of Christ.

12 For our struggle is not against flesh and blood, but against the rulers, against the authorities, against the powers of this dark world and against the spiritual forces of evil in the heavenly realms. 13 Therefore put on the full armor of God, so that when the day of evil comes, you may be able to stand your ground, and after you have done everything, to stand. 14 Stand firm then, with the belt of truth buckled around your waist, with the breastplate of righteousness in place, 15 and with your feet fitted with the readiness that comes from the gospel of peace.
Ephesians 6:12-15 (NIV)

Do be afraid of these demonic powers and principalities, Jesus made a public spectacle of them on the cross.

15 When He had disarmed the rulers and authorities [those supernatural forces of evil operating against us], He made a public example of them [exhibiting them as captives in His triumphal procession], having triumphed over them through the cross.
Colossians 2:14-16

Be bold and courageous because they (the demonic powers and authorities) are essentially captives; you are the victor who is unaware of your power and authority over the enemy that is holding you captive. The enemy triumphs when we live uninformed or ignorant of the power that has been made available to us. Today is the day to make a conscious decision to wield the hammer of God's word, the sword of the spirit, begin at the roots and hack at that stronghold relentlessly, as you do you will walk in greater freedom and victory.

*It is for freedom that Christ has set us free. Stand firm, then, and do not let yourselves be burdened **again** by a yoke of slavery.*
Galatians 5:1(NIV)

The Greek word for again is **palin** and it means repetition of action. Do not continue to repeat the same action that Christ delivered you from. This is the day to get back up righteous man of God, woman of God. We have no time to waste staying down, arise and take territories from our common enemy. God in His word made room for our rising, so let's help one another to rise back up as well.

Brothers, if anyone is caught in any sin, you who are spiritual [that is, you who are responsive to the guidance of the Spirit] are to restore such a person in a spirit of <u>gentleness</u> [not with a sense of superiority or self-righteousness], keeping a watchful eye on yourself, so that you are not tempted as well.
Galatians 6:1(AMP)

Soldiers do not leave a fallen comrade on the battlefield to become a POW (prisoner of war) to the enemy. They endeavor to rescue the individuals. Even amidst crossfire, they promptly transport their wounded to medical personnel for treatment to restore them back to health. The same applies to our fellow Christians. When we encounter a fallen brother in Christ, we should not point fingers or say, "I told you so."

The word gentleness is the Greek word **prautes** defined as humility, meekness. We should humbly restore, mend, repair such a one bearing in mind that sometimes the devil can ask permission to sift us. What if that brother or sister whose downfall we witnessed, may just have been agitated by the devil to the verge of overthrowing their faith with permission from God, would we be quick to judge them or would we turn our plates and intercede for them to enter their season of correction (restoration) unto righteousness?

If we know that:

[16] *"God so [greatly] loved and dearly prized the world, that He [even] gave His [One and] only begotten Son, so that whoever believes and trusts in Him [as Savior] shall not perish but have eternal life.*
John 3:16 (AMP)

We would not continue to take His mercy and Grace for granted. Our salvation came at a great price – the death and sacrifice of our Lord and savior on the cross.

Job 14:7-9 (NIV) says,

"For there is hope for a tree,
If it is cut down, that it will sprout again, And that its tender
shoots will not cease. ⁸ Though its root may grow old in the
earth, And its stump may die in the ground,
⁹ Yet at the scent of water it will bud And bring forth branches
like a plant.

When a tree is cut above the ground, its future may appear bleak. The tree may look dead, and its roots may grow old and whither but as long as it has a root, at the scent of water that tree will live again. That tells me that there is hope for a habitual sinner, the devil may have taken the reins you surrendered to him and used it to spin your life out of control. You may feel hopeless like a dead tree but at the scent of the water of the word of God, you will arise and be reacquainted with the love of our Father. The Father who would leave the 99 to find the one lost sheep. The Father who would rejoice and throw a party for the returned prodigal son. The Father with arms opened wide, unquestioning and ready to restore you to your rightful place when you decide to take a step home.

Please bow your head with me and repeat this prayer out loud:

Father God, I come before you in all humility to ask forgiveness of every sin I committed that brought you pain and kept me far from your love and healing. According to 1 John 1:9, you said If we confess our sins, You are faithful and just to forgive us our sins and to cleanse us from all unrighteousness. I confess and renounce these sins (confess your sins to God), I denounce them and ask that you would not only forgive me but make it like it never happened by cleansing me from all unrighteousness with the blood of Jesus. I now renew my covenant to serve you and to make Jesus Christ Lord over my entire life. I break every agreement I made with Satan through living a lifestyle of sin. I demolish every demonic stronghold in my life and ask Father according to your word in Amos 2:9 that you would destroy its root below the ground and its fruits above the ground. I arise as a warrior with the armor of God and with the power and authority that Jesus gave me to cast out unclean spirits. I command the spirit of iniquity to leave me now and never return. I surrender to the work of the Holy Spirit and invite Him to fill and use me completely, to rule, reign and have dominion over me. I am yours Lord, now and forever in Jesus name, amen.

CHAPTER FIVE

THE SEASON OF INSTRUCTION IN RIGHTEOUSNESS PT.1

*"All scripture is given by inspiration of God, and is profitable for doctrine, for reproof, for correction, for **instruction** in righteousness: [17] That the man of God may be perfect, thoroughly furnished unto all good works.*

2 Timothy 3:16-17 (KJV)

This season is the longest chapter I wrote in this book, so I split it into two chapters. I asked the Holy Ghost why that is the case. I sensed in my spirit it is because we will camp out in this season till Jesus comes. Each "season" represents a distinct phase in our spiritual journey, marked by unique challenges and opportunities for growth. We started off with a season focused on doctrine, during which we studied the scriptures and stored them in our heart. This is followed by a season of reproof, where the word and our faith are tested to examine its genuineness. Should we fall short or found wanting, the season of correction facilitates rectification and personal restoration. Ultimately, through the season of instruction, we are guided towards virtuous living and encouraged to exemplify spiritual principles in our daily lives.

The Greek word for instruction is **paideia,** which means tutorage, the whole training and education of children that includes nurturing, correction, discipline and instruction. Instruction which aims at increasing virtue.

As a parent, I have the responsibility of teaching my child right from wrong, guiding, nurturing, correcting, providing and protecting him. When he does not adhere to our household rules, I administer appropriate disciplinary measures to hopefully make him see the error of his ways and correct the behavior. The goal is to train him to become a more responsible adult, to one day be a contributing member of society, a great husband and father. So, I must look beyond his present and make plans for his future.

♦ *The season of instruction in righteousness is a season of full submission to the training of the Holy Spirit, so we can grow in virtue and reflect God to the world.*

We will explore in depth the four ways that the word of God is profitable to us in the season of instruction in righteousness. They are for training, nurturing, disciplinary correction (chastisement and chastening), and discipline.

1. **Training:**

> *"My son, do not make light of the discipline (paideia) of the LORD, and do not lose heart and give up when you are corrected by Him. ⁶For the Lord disciplines (paideuo)and corrects those whom He loves, and He punishes every son whom He receives and welcomes (to His heart). ⁷You must submit to [correction for the*

purpose of] discipline (paideia); God is dealing with
you as with sons; for¹what son is there whom his
father does not discipline (paideia)?
Hebrews 12:5b-7 (AMP)

The Greek word for discipline in this scripture is also
paideia, the same word that means instruction – education
and training. I used to think that the discipline in this
scripture meant disciplinary correction but that is not the
case. The LORD – Jehovah the self-existent one is presented
here as our tutor. He loves us dearly; He is fond of us. He is
pleased with us, so He trains and instructs us to grow in
virtue and reflect Him to the world.

Hebrews 12:5 above admonishes us not to make light of the
Lord's discipline (training). The word make light or regard
lightly is **Oligoreo** – meaning to have little regard, to
disesteem, to despise (feel contempt, to look down on), to
turn a deaf ear, to look the other way.

But doom to you who fight your Maker— you're a pot at odds
with the potter! Does clay talk back to the potter: 'What are
you doing? What clumsy fingers!'
Isaiah 45:9 (MSG)

We are the clay; He is the potter. The clay does not question
the potter. The clay stays pliable in the hands of the potter
and allows the potter to mold it into a vessel fit for the
master's use. We should not despise the Lord's training;
instead, we should heed it, respect it, prefer it, desire it,

favor it, and submit to it. Why? Because of the harvest it produces.

> [11] No _discipline_ (paideia) seems pleasant at the time, but painful. Later on, however, it produces a harvest of righteousness and peace for those who have been trained by it.
> **Hebrews 12:11 (AMP)**

No discipline – **_paideia_ (training)** seems pleasant, joyful, enjoyable in the moment but later if we submit to it, undergo it, stay under it, persevere in it, and let it do the internal work required to refine us, we will reap a harvest of righteousness and peace. He will mold us into His image, make us what He wants us to be, and do what we were created to do. The scripture assures us of a harvest of righteousness which in Greek is **dikaiosyne** defined as integrity, virtue, purity of life, rightness, correctness of thinking, feeling, and acting, justification. God's training aims to shape us into people of integrity who practice (live) what they preach. This is the purpose for this season.

While Jesus was alive, he played the role of tutor to his disciples. Aside from his many parables and sermons, he also taught them how to pray, how to love, He provided them with fish when he showed them where to cast their net, he paid their tax (Matthew 17:27), he protected them in the storm while out and about on the boat, he defended them before the Pharisees and Sadducees. He made provision ahead of time for Peter's restoration because He knew that if Peter had stayed in a fallen situation, it would have devastated their faith. Most of all He was their friend. When He was getting ready to leave, He told his disciples that He would not leave them as orphans, He would ask the Father to give them another advocate to help them and be with them forever – the Spirit of Truth. For there to be another advocate, means they had an advocate prior. Jesus was their advocate. When he died, they were heart broken, grieving and in sorrow. When the "another advocate" came on the scene, they were filled with boldness, they were equipped to proclaim the gospel. The Holy Spirit did in them what Jesus promised He would do.

26 But the Helper (Comforter, Advocate, Intercessor— Counselor, Strengthener, Standby), the Holy Spirit, whom the Father will send in My name [in My place, to represent Me and act on My behalf], He will teach you all things. And He will help you remember everything that I have told you.
John 14:26 (AMP)

Aside from being their AIC[2] (advocate, intercessor, comforter, counselor), the Holy Spirit's job was to teach them all things and remind them everything Jesus had taught them. **Didasko** is the Greek word for teach meaning to impart instruction, to conduct oneself as a teacher, to explain or expound a thing. People marveled at Peter's sermon on the day of Pentecost. They knew the disciples to be simple ordinary fishermen, but when the Spirit of truth came upon them, they became different men.

13 Now when the men of the Sanhedrin (Jewish High Court) saw the confidence and boldness of Peter and John, and

grasped the fact that they were uneducated and untrained [ordinary] men, they were astounded, and began to recognize that they had <u>been</u> with Jesus.
Acts 4:13(AMP)

When you make a habit of spending time with the Lord in prayer and in His word, it shows. You receive a deposit of His glory that makes you think and talk differently. You radiate boldness and supernatural courage. You have the "I've been with Jesus glow."

Moses had that glow when he returned from mount Sinai. He had spent 40 days with God without food or water conversing with God and documenting the words of the covenant.

[29] When Moses came down from Mount Sinai with the two tablets of the Testimony in his hand, he did not know that the skin of his face was shining [with a unique radiance] <u>because he had been speaking with God</u>. [30] When Aaron and all the Israelites saw Moses, behold, the skin of his face shone, and they were afraid to approach him.
Exodus 34:29-30 (AMP)

Moses face was radiant because he had been speaking with God. Have you been with Jesus lately? Life can get very busy, mine certainly has. It took grief to make me slow down and take a sit in His presence to figure out who I was and what He called me to be and to do somewhat.

When Jesus visited Bethany, it was Martha that opened her home to Jesus. After she welcomed Him in, she got busy. Let's sit here for a minute and imagine this scene. Jesus arrived in Bethany accompanied by His followers, and Martha recognized an opportunity. She took it, she invited Him in. Jesus did not give notice that He was coming so Martha could not prepare them food before Jesus arrived Bethany. She seized the moment to host the King of Glory in her home.

38 Now while they were on their way, Jesus entered a village [called Bethany], and a woman named Martha welcomed Him into her home. 39 She had a sister named Mary, who seated herself at the Lord's feet and was continually listening to His teaching. 40 But Martha was very busy and distracted with all of her serving responsibilities; and she approached Him and said, "Lord, is it of no concern to You that my sister has left me to do the serving alone? Tell her to help me and do her part." 41 But the Lord replied to her, "Martha, Martha, you are worried and bothered and anxious about so many things; 42 but only one thing is necessary, for Mary has chosen the good part [that which is to her advantage], which will not be taken away from her."
Luke 10:38-42 (AMP)

Martha is in the kitchen cooking up a storm, she probably called Jesus' mama to find out His favorite dish (that's what I would do), just doing her best to entertain and care for her guest. This was not Mary's house, she should be helping her sister in the kitchen, but Mary is observed listening attentively at His feet, absorbing the teachings of life that emanate from the lips of the one who embodies the word in the flesh. For her, this experience could not be more fulfilling. When Martha complained that Mary was not helping with the preparation, the Lord said that Mary had chosen the good part.

Agathos is the Greek word for good meaning useful, excellent, benefit. Mary made an excellent choice, and it will not be taken away from her or cut off. There was nothing wrong with what Martha was doing, she was taking care of her guest. But this was no ordinary guest.

This was a guest who did not have long to live, a guest who wanted to prep his followers for missionary work and needed them to hear His words because those words would sustain them in the tumultuous days that would soon follow. This was God.

When we accepted Jesus as Lord, our body became His temple, a home for his dwelling. Like Martha, we invite Him in and then we get too busy to sit and build intimacy with Him. I find myself to be just like Martha, worried, bothered, and anxious about many things. But one thing is necessary, one thing is needful, one thing is worth being concerned about and that is what Mary chose. To sit and attend to the teaching of her Savior. What father is not elated when their children come home, set aside their phone and all social media and say, "dad, I just want to spend time with you today." Imagine how God would feel if we did that, if we give Him all our attention and surrender to our season of instruction (training). He will guide us and help us develop into mature Christians who are prepared for the deeper understanding of the Scriptures. God's training is not for the weak of heart.

What does surrendering look like? It is setting aside our own will and setting our minds to go deeper in Him by spending more time in His presence and in His word. When He says fast, you fast. When He says turn off that show on TV, you do because you know that in your obedience lies your protection. When we live in His presence, life feels lighter because we are no longer burdened by the cares of this world, we are about your father's business. Ephesians 3:20 says that:

> *God is able (He has the ability, the resources) to do superabundantly more than all that we dare to ask (require, call for, desire, crave) or think (perceive, understand) beyond our hopes or dreams according to His power that is at work (active, operative) within us.*

How much God can do is predicated on how much we allow Him to do. When we plug into the Holy Spirit, we receive spiritual downloads.

> [9] *But as it is written: "Eye has not seen, nor ear heard, Nor have entered into the heart of man*
> *The things which God has prepared for those who love Him."*
> **1 Corinthians 2:9(NKJV)**

10 For God has revealed them to us through the Holy Spirit; for the Spirit searches all things (diligently) even (sounding and measuring) the (profound) depths of God (the divine counsels and things far beyond human understanding). 11 For what person knows the thoughts and motives of a man except the man's spirit within him? So also no one knows the <u>thoughts</u> *of God except the Spirit of God.*
1 Corinthians 2:10-11 (AMP)

The Holy Spirit is the best trainer that we can ask for in our walk with God. He knows God's thoughts (opinions, view, idea, perception, feelings, understanding). We can ask Him His thoughts regarding any decision we plan to make.

My prayer life used to be me making a laundry list of what I am believing God for, finding a scripture that lines up with those things and then rattling them off before God in prayer. I appeared before God with my own agenda. Well, I don't think that is what Jesus meant in John 16:23 (AMP) when He said,

"whatsoever you ask the Father in my name (as My representative), He will give it to you."

When we do not receive what we ask for, we chug it down to maybe God said later or He said no. We need to correct course. Can you imagine the time and heartache we would save ourselves If we spent time seeking his thoughts or inquiring about His will before engaging in the pursuit of the promise or going on that fast. James 4:3 (AMP) says,

3 You ask [God for something] and do not receive it, because you ask [a]with wrong motives [out of selfishness or with an unrighteous agenda], so that [when you get what you want] you may spend it on your [hedonistic] desires.

Since the Spirit knows the thoughts of God and He is our tutor, what if we changed our approach to prayer by making it God directed instead of man directed, God guided instead of flesh motivated. David practiced this approach a lot. He would inquire of the Lord before making any decision. 1 Samuel 23:9-12 (NIV):

⁹ When David learned that Saul was plotting against him, he said to Abiathar the priest, "Bring the ephod." ¹⁰ David said, "Lord, God of Israel, your servant has heard definitely that Saul plans to come to Keilah and destroy the town on account of me. ¹¹ Will the citizens of Keilah surrender me to him?

Will Saul come down, as your servant has heard? Lord, God of Israel, tell your servant."

And the Lord said, "He will."

¹² Again David asked, "Will the citizens of Keilah surrender me and my men to Saul?"

And the Lord said, "They will."

¹³ So David and his men, about six hundred in number, left Keilah and kept moving from place to place. When Saul was told that David had escaped from Keilah, he did not go there.
1 Samuel 23:9-12 (NIV)

Let's give background to this story. David had just delivered the people of Keilah from the hands of the Philistines so it was expected that they would express their gratitude by protecting him from Saul. David did not assume that they would help him because he knew men could flip on him in an instant. David did not immediately go to God in prayer to ask to help him battle King Saul, even though Saul was no longer anointed by God he was still in the office of a King.

In that situation, I would get on my knees and ask God to help me win the battle against an enemy who was coming for me or show me where to run. But not David, his first inquiry was to verify from God if what he heard about Saul coming to destroy him was true. David's questions to God were very specific and he made the decision to leave the city with his men based on the answers God gave him. He did not sit in a corner to bemoan his situation which he had the right to do because God not only confirmed Saul's plan, but He also revealed to David the heart of the citizens of Keilah because he took the time to inquire.

In the medical field, we use SBAR for communication. You first start with the situation (what is going on right now), background (or history to give context), the assessment (what you think the problem is), and finally the recommendation or request (what you want done or think should be done). In our prayers, we often SBAR God—we give Him a heads up on the situation, provide the background, describe the problem, and then proceed to tell Him what we want Him to do. However, a more fitting approach is SBAQ: Situation, Background, Assessment, and Question (what should I do, what do you think, how should I approach this situation?). By shifting from requests to questions, we acknowledge our limited understanding and invite guidance, fostering a more humble and open relationship with God. This change encourages us to seek His wisdom, aligning our hearts with His will and direction rather than simply presenting our demands. For instance, instead of saying, "God, please fix this problem," you might say, "God, this is the situation I'm facing; here's the background and my assessment—what do you think I should do next?" Using SBAQ as a framework not only transforms our communication with God but also deepens our spiritual connection by demonstrating trust and openness to His counsel.

Employing the SBAQ approach in prayer involves patiently waiting for a response from God and actively listening, rather than departing immediately after praying. Not long after my divorce was finalized, I found myself navigating a wave of new challenges. My tenant unexpectedly broke their lease and left my property without warning, compounding the uncertainty I already felt. With months passing and no new tenants in sight, I was left covering both the rent on my condo and the mortgage on my now-vacant house—my savings dwindled each month, and anxiety crept in. I decided to list the house for both sale and rent, thinking whichever happened first would relieve my burden. This seemed like the logical path, but beneath the surface, I felt hopeless, praying, and fasting for a breakthrough, yet feeling the tension between faith and fear.

Throughout this period, my prayers often followed the familiar pattern of laying out my situation, recounting the background, and pleading, "God, please help me sell or rent this house." I quoted every scripture I could recall about God's provision and faithfulness. I even drove out to the house—an hour and a half from where I lived—to anoint it, pray over it, and declare that it was a blessing, not a curse. I would say to my house, "you are a blessing from God and so you cannot add sorrow by depleting my savings account because the blessing of God maketh rich and He adds no sorrow (Proverbs 10:22)." Despite all this, each day felt like a balancing act between hope and anxiety; I watched my savings drop and wrestled with growing doubt.

Then, one seemingly ordinary morning at work, a coworker struck up a conversation that quietly shifted my perspective. He mentioned his own long commute and casually noted that he lived near my house. At first, I didn't think much of the coincidence, but his words lingered. That interaction planted a seed. It made me realize that while the commute seemed daunting to me, others navigated similar situations every day. It was as if God was gently nudging me, hinting at an option I hadn't considered.

A couple of weeks before my house listing agreement was due to expire, I entered a period of fasting—not specifically about the house, but regarding another project weighing on my heart. During prayer, I shifted my approach. Instead of asking God to fix things my way, I surrendered and asked, "God, what are Your thoughts?" Immediately, I felt compelled to bring up my house in prayer, something I hadn't planned. I asked God directly for His perspective—should I keep pushing to sell or rent, or was there another way? Although I didn't hear an audible answer, I experienced a deep knowing, a clarity that I should move back into my house. It was a surprising thought; one I had never genuinely entertained until that moment.

At first, I practically tried to argue: my house, though larger and newer with space for our dog, was an hour's drive from both my job and my son's school. The prospect of a long commute seemed overwhelming, and I felt the familiar grip of anxiety. But as I sat with the conviction, I noticed something remarkable—a profound peace, the kind Scripture describes as passing all understanding, began to settle over me. The timing was perfect because my lease at the condo and my house listing agreement were both expiring the following month, which coincided with the month that schools will be closed for summer, and I worked only 3 days a week. The fear and uncertainty that had dogged me for months lifted, replaced by a calm assurance that this was the path I was meant to take.

Bolstered by this peace, I began taking concrete steps forward. I spoke with my son's father, and together we agreed on a new parenting schedule that would allow both of us to remain in our homes without disrupting our son's routine or school. Simultaneously, I researched hospitals near my house and found one just fifteen minutes away, realizing I could reasonably cut my commute if needed. Each decision felt less daunting as I leaned into the peace God had given me. The clarity and calm I felt began to influence my daily life—I was more patient with myself and others, more hopeful about the future, and more grounded in my faith. Even obstacles that once felt insurmountable seemed manageable now, filtered through the lens of God's provision and presence.

Looking back, I see how the SBAQ approach—pausing to ask God's thoughts rather than simply presenting requests—transformed my decision-making. My faith wasn't just a backdrop; it became the very foundation for practical action. Moving back into my house wasn't the answer I expected, but it was the answer I needed. Now, a month after relocating, I know I am exactly where I am supposed to be. Aligning my actions with God's direction has brought a sense of contentment and hope I hadn't felt in a long time. The boundary lines truly fell for me in pleasant places as soon as I aligned with God's thoughts.

⁶ The boundary lines have fallen for me in pleasant places; surely I have a delightful inheritance.
⁷ I will praise the Lord, who counsels me; even at night my heart instructs me. ⁸ I keep my eyes always on the Lord. With him at my right hand, I will not be shaken.
Psalm 16:6-8 (NIV)

It takes time and patience to sit at His feet and ask His thoughts. The Psalmist said above "I will praise the Lord who counsels me." **Yaas** is the Hebrew word for counsel it means to advise, consult, give counsel, guide, plan. Viewing prayer as a form of consultation with God can lead to a shift in perspective. Engaging with God in prayer before making decisions allows us to seek guidance thoughtfully. It would require going beyond His gates (which we enter with thanksgiving) and entering His courts (with praise) – Psalm 100:4 and then sit at His feet to inquire or consult Him.

In 2 Kings 3:8-20 when the King of Israel, the King of Judah and the King of Edom were in the wilderness of Edom on their way to battle the King of Moab, they ran into a lack of water situation. They feared they would be delivered into the hands of their enemy. Their first instinct was to look for a prophet who would inquire of the Lord for them. Elisha, when called upon to inquire (the Hebrew word *daras* – to question, to consult) of the Lord would not prophecy without worship first. When the minstrel played, the hand of the Lord came upon Elisha, and he prophesied that they would not see wind nor rain, yet the valley shall be filled with water for them to drink and this is but a light thing for the Lord to do and it came to pass as he had prophesied.

Whatever obstacles or challenges you might be facing right now, remember it is but a light thing for the Lord to do. Adopting an inquiring or consultative approach to prayer shifts our prayer from an individual focus to a collective one, as we intercede for the concerns that the Spirit of God impresses upon our hearts. Our dreams and visions are all connected, and the Holy Spirit can see and make those connections even when we cannot see what lies in front of us. Ananias obedience to the revelation he received from God in a vision led to Paul's conversion which led to the conversion of multitudes of gentiles via Paul's missionary work. Hannah wanted a baby, God needed a prophet. Her obedience to give her son to the service of God placed her in alignment with the will of God on earth as it is in heaven.

Hannah surrendered her womb to God and in the process received her miracle while God received a faithful priest who did according to what was in His heart and in His mind.

During the Instruction season, God develops our character to reflect His nature, focusing more on who we are than what we do, since He made us in His likeness. In the garden, whatever Adam named an animal, that name became its official designation. He did this by acting according to the image of God and exercising the authority granted to him by God. God could trust his heart and allowed whatever he said to be so, because they were one.

> [17] But whoever is united with the Lord is one with him in spirit.
> **1 Corinthians 6:17(NIV)**

God is calling us to unity with His Spirit, to a life of oneness. Speaking about Abraham in Genesis 18:17, God said, "shall I hide from Abraham what I am about to do?" Abraham was His friend, God involved him in His plans. God yearns to have that type of relationship with us, where He can freely share His agenda with us but that can only come from a place of oneness and trust. Can God trust you with His plan and purpose? Can we make the time to sit and inquire from Him?

♦ *The fruit of the season of instruction (training) is oneness with God.*

In Antioch, the apostles were initially referred to as Christians due to their adherence to the teachings of Christ. When the church in Jerusalem heard that the Church at Antioch were preaching and converting Greeks to Christ, they sent Barnabas to investigate. This is the description of Barnabas:

[24] For Barnabas was a good man [privately and publicly—his godly character benefited both himself and others] and he was full of the Holy Spirit and full of faith [in Jesus the Messiah, through whom believers have everlasting life]. And a great number of people were brought to the Lord.
Acts 11:24 (AMP)

Barnabas is referred to as a good man. Here is that word again **agathos** – good, pleasant, agreeable, joyful, happy, excellent, distinguished, upright, honorable in public and private. We encountered this word earlier when Jesus mentioned that Mary had chosen the good part. Barnabas's godly character benefited himself, others, and God, drawing many to the Lord. It was neither his preaching nor his teaching, but his character served as evidence, demonstrating that he had been in the presence of Jesus. He was full of the Spirit and full of faith. The word full is the Greek word **pleres** meaning filled up, complete, lacking nothing, perfect, covered over.

◆ *The season of instruction (training) in righteousness promotes godly character in us that draws men to God.*

As believers in Christ, we are servants of God and God has given us the ministry of reconciling men to him not in words alone but in deeds as well.

18 All this is from God, who reconciled us to himself through Christ and gave us the ministry of reconciliation: 19 that God was reconciling the world to himself in Christ, not counting people's sins against them. And he has committed to us the message of reconciliation. 20 We are therefore Christ's ambassadors, as though God were making his appeal through us. We implore you on Christ's behalf: Be reconciled to God.
2 Corinthians 5:18-20 (NIV)

Katallage the Greek word for reconciliation means to restore to divine favor. We have the ministry of restoring mankind to God's favor, drawing men back to God, mending the broken relationship between God and man just as Christ did for us. An ambassador is an official representative of a foreign country who is not bound by the laws of the host country but subject to the laws of their home country. An ambassador undergoes training, holds a degree, may speak several languages, holds a stellar reputation, stives to maintain good relationship between the foreign country and his own. We are God's ambassadors – his representatives on earth, we are in the world, but we are not of this world. This world is not our home, we are citizens of heaven. We are God's mouthpiece; we are His enforcers. We enforce His authority upon this earth through the words of our mouth and our godly character.

15 Timothy, do everything you can to present yourself to God as a man who is fully genuine, a worker unashamed of your mission, a guide capable of leading others along the correct path defined by the word of truth.
2 Timothy 2:15 (VOICE)

As an ambassador of God, our mission if we should accept is to lead others along the correct path to the only one who is the way, the truth and the life. For this call, we are held to a higher standard, we do not conform to the pattern of this world. We do not need a pulpit to carry out this assignment. We can reconcile our children, our neighbors, co-workers, our bus driver, everyone in our part of the world to God not with words alone but with a demonstration of our godly character.

Your very lives are a letter that anyone can read by just looking at you. Christ himself wrote it—not with ink, but with God's living Spirit; not chiseled into stone, but carved into human lives—and we publish it.
2 Corinthians 3:2-3 (MSG)

Some people may never open their bible to read about God, but they can read us - they will form their perspectives through observing our actions and behavior. We are a living walking love letter from Christ to the world. Jesus asked his disciples, "who do men say that I am." His disciples replied, "John the Baptist (Jesus was fearless in his preaching like John was), Elijah (Jesus did raise the dead like Elijah did), one of the prophets."

Who do men say you are? Meditate on that for a minute. Reflecting on how others see us can offer valuable insights into our relationships and self-awareness. Our godly character should speak louder than our words so that men may be won over to God. This is why we were created, we should live each day intentionally with our values at the forefront, making every minute count to the glory of God.

[11] Thou art worthy, O Lord, to receive glory and honour and power: for thou hast created all things, and for thy pleasure they are and were created.
Revelation 4:11 (KJV)

We were created to serve God's pleasure, will, purpose, decree, desire. As God's ambassadors, we serve at His pleasure, and we are tasked with the duty of carrying out heaven's agenda upon the earth. If this is the case, how will we know God's day-to-day agenda if we do not spend daily time in His presence to inquire? If we approach God with our own agenda, then it defeats the purpose of serving at His pleasure which is why we were created. If we approach life with this mindset, it would be easier to take life's difficulties to God because it is technically His problem. Just as ambassadors represent their home country, believers are called to represent God's interests on earth. This parallel helps illustrate our responsibilities and privileges as God's ambassadors.

In the natural, an ambassador serves at the pleasure of their president, reporting problems to their home government and receiving instruction and support in response. In much the same way, we're encouraged to bring all our challenges, plans, projects, and decisions before God—our heavenly "home government"—and rely on His guidance, support, and protection.

The privileges of being God's ambassadors include His promise of protection and provision. Just as a natural ambassador has a security detail, we have spiritual protection against the attacks of the enemy: God's angels, the authority in Jesus' name, and His word—the sword of the Spirit, the blood of Jesus—guard us as we fulfill our mission here on earth. Serving at God's pleasure is not just a duty; it's an invitation to live with purpose, supported by God's presence and empowered to expand His influence through our daily choices.

2. Nurturing:

To nurture is to take care of, feed, and protect someone or something, especially young children or plants, and help him, her, or it to develop.

2 like newborn babies [you should] long for the pure milk of the word, so that by it you may be nurtured and <u>grow</u> in respect to salvation [its ultimate fulfillment],
1 Peter 2:2 (AMP)

Auxano is the Greek word for grow meaning to increase, become greater, inward Christian growth, enlarge. The nurturing we receive from the milk of the word helps us to grow and deepen our experience of salvation or to make it greater. Our free salvation was bought and paid for with the blood of Jesus Christ. **Soteria** the Greek word for salvation encompasses deliverance, salvation, safety, preservation, and health. Increasing in our salvation means living in the fullness of what Jesus accomplished for us and experiencing everything He saved us from. Jesus gave us authority to cast out demons, heal the sick, and to trample on snakes and scorpions. Walking in the authority and power that Jesus has given us can only come when we nourish our soul with His word of truth that brings knowledge, wisdom, and enlightenment. Furthermore, this nourishment brings knowledge, wisdom, and enlightenment, enabling us to walk confidently in the promises of God.

¹² So then, my dear ones, just as you have always obeyed [my instructions with enthusiasm], not only in my presence, but now much more in my absence, continue to work out your salvation [that is, cultivate it, bring it to full effect, actively pursue spiritual maturity] with awe-inspired fear and trembling [using serious caution and critical self-evaluation to avoid anything that might offend God or discredit the name of Christ]. ¹³ For it is [not your strength, but it is] God who is effectively at work in you, both to will and to work [that is, strengthening, energizing, and creating in you the longing and the ability to fulfill your purpose] for His good pleasure.
Philippians 2:12-13 (AMP)

While on earth we can fully work out our salvation - to continue to grow in the knowledge of our Lord Jesus Christ and in our faith. Faith comes by hearing and hearing by the word of God (Romans 10:17). If you struggle with moral weakness for instance, consider studying God's word on purity and the power of the cross to resurrect you from sin to show that you are a workman who has no reason to be ashamed but rightly divides the word of truth in your area of need. That is how we are nourished by the word.

There is room to grow in our salvation. There is room for more, we can believe God for more because we are meant for more. The good news is that we do not have to do it with our own strength. Verse 13 above says that our God strengthens, energizes us, and creates in us the longing and ability to work out our salvation for His good pleasure. Psalm 35:27 says that God delights in the prosperity of His servants. God is pleased when we live victorious and prosperous lives, and use our resources to expand His influence, show His love, and help others reconnect with Him. What a good father He is.

³ He humbled you and allowed you to be hungry and fed you with manna, [a substance] which you did not know, nor did your fathers know, so that He might make you understand [by personal experience] that man does not live by bread alone, but man lives by every word that proceeds out of the mouth of the LORD.
Deuteronomy 8:3 (AMP)

Haya is the Hebrew word for lives meaning sustain life, to revive from sickness, from discouragement, from faintness, from death, to restore to health, to restore to life, repair, be whole, nourish up, quicken, recover. Man is first a spirit, living in a body and possesses a soul.

While our physical bodies require food for strength and health, our spirit is sustained, healed, encouraged, repaired, nourished, and revived by every word that proceeds from the mouth of God. We were not created to be satisfied with only earthly food or physical fulfillment. In the same way that we seek medical help when our bodies are unwell, our spirits yearn for restoration through unity with the God who made us in His image and likeness.

Just as a tree draws life from streams of water, our innermost being thrives on the living word of God, which is described in Psalm 119:103 as "sweeter than honey and the drippings of the honeycomb." Without this spiritual nourishment, our spirits become dry and unsatisfied, no matter what else we pursue.

David said it best in Psalm 63:

> *God—you're my God! I can't get enough of you!*
> *I've worked up such hunger and thirst for God,*
> *traveling across dry and weary deserts.*
> *²⁻⁴ So here I am in the place of worship, eyes open,*
> *drinking in your strength and glory.*
> **Psalm 63:1-4 (MSG)**

By drawing on God's word and letting it permeate every aspect of ourselves, we become like a flourishing tree— strong, whole, and filled with life.

Our heavenly father not only provides us with spiritual bread through His word, but He also provides nourishment for our physical bodies much like a parent provides for their children. For instance, when the Israelites were hungry in the wilderness, God miraculously sent quail and rained bread from heaven for forty years to feed them and demonstrate His care. This act of provision reflects God's nurturing character, which is further revealed in His name, El Shaddai, found in Genesis 17. The term "El Shaddai" is often translated as "God Almighty," but it also carries the meaning "the breasted one." This imagery speaks to God's role as a source of nourishment, comfort, protection, and sustenance—just as a mother's breast provides for a child. In introducing Himself as El Shaddai to Abraham, God was emphasizing His ability and willingness to nurture, sustain, and meet every need, even in times of uncertainty and journeying into the unknown.

Transitioning to the teachings of Jesus, we see this same theme of provision echoed in the Lord's Prayer in Matthew 6:11. After honoring God and seeking His will, Jesus teaches His disciples to ask, "Give us this day our daily bread," highlighting that our daily nourishment—both physical and spiritual—comes from God. This theme of God as provider is interwoven throughout scripture, reminding us again and again that our needs matter to Him.

Jesus reinforced this lesson by reintroducing God's nurturing nature to His followers, preparing them for the miracles of provision that would come, such as the feeding of the multitudes in Matthew 14.

[14] When Jesus landed and saw a large crowd, he had compassion on them and healed their sick. [15] As evening approached, the disciples came to him and said, "This is a remote place, and it's already getting late. Send the crowds

away, so they can go to the villages and buy themselves
some food." [16] Jesus replied, "They do not need to go away.
You give them something to eat."
Matthew 14: 14-16 (NIV)

Jesus provided both spiritual and physical nourishment to the crowd to emphasize that El Shaddai, the God of Abraham, remains constant throughout time and can address their physical needs as well. It is likely that Jesus instructed his disciples to feed the crowd because he had previously taught them to seek daily bread from God when He taught them how to pray. From Abraham, who trusted God while venturing into unfamiliar territory, to the Israelites receiving manna in the desert, and later to the disciples learning to rely on God for sustenance, the Bible consistently shows that believing in God's care leads to having our needs met.

In our region, food resources are more plentiful compared to many developing countries that are food deserts. Growing up with a single mother in West Africa, my family faced significant financial hardship. There were times when we wore used clothing and, on some days, barely had enough food to eat. Some evenings, my mother would quietly go without dinner so that we could have a small meal. Through all these struggles, we depended on Elshaddai to sustain us and meet our daily needs. True to His nature, He came through for us, offering comfort and provision when we needed it most.

As we reflect on these stories, we can be encouraged that the same God who provided for Abraham, the Israelites, and the disciples is actively caring for us today. The assurance is clear: when we trust in God and rely on Him, our daily spiritual and physical needs will be met. His nurturing nature invites us to come to Him with confidence, knowing that He delights in providing for His children.

David said in Psalm 145:15-16 (AMP):

[15] The eyes of all look to You [in hopeful expectation], And You give them their food in due time. [16] You open Your hand And satisfy the desire of every living thing.

3. Disciplinary Correction:

In educational settings, if a student displays behavior that is contrary to the institution's code of conduct or disrupts the learning environment, disciplinary measures may be implemented to address the issue. In much the same way that educators seek to guide students toward better behavior, spiritual discipline is intended to guide believers toward personal growth. Similarly, during our time of spiritual training (tutorage) under the guidance of the Lord, when we sin, disciplinary correction is administered out of love with the aim of fostering growth and positive change, rather than as a form of punishment.

[24] He who withholds the rod [of discipline] hates his son, But he who loves him disciplines and trains him diligently and appropriately [with wisdom and love].
Proverbs 13:24 (AMP)

Musar is the Hebrew word for discipline – to warn, correct, discipline, rebuke, instruct. The word love is Hebrew word *ahab* meaning human love to another, God's love toward man. Parents discipline (musar) their children out of love (ahab) to correct, guide and build their character. It never feels good in the moment but if we are consistent with it the reward is invaluable. We are commanded to discipline our children to save their soul.

[13] Do not withhold discipline from the child;
If you swat him with a reed-like rod [applied with godly wisdom], he will not die.
[14] You shall swat him with the reed-like rod
And rescue his life from Sheol (the nether world, the place of the dead).
Proverbs 23:13-14 (AMP)

An approach that is effective for one child may not necessarily be suitable for another. Taking away my son's electronic devices gets his attention and promotes godly sorrow that is equal to none. By 'godly sorrow,' I mean a genuine feeling of remorse that leads to positive change, rather than mere regret or fear of punishment. I correct and discipline my son because I love him. I would refrain from disciplining my neighbor's child should I witness any misbehavior, provided the situation does not pose any risk of harm. This is because I believe it is not within my authority to intervene in such matters. I may inform his parents of his behavior and allow them to determine an appropriate course of action. Just as parents' discipline their children out of love and concern for their growth, so too does our heavenly father discipline us to build up our godly character because we belong to Him and He loves us. Remember that our obedience to His will is more important than our sacrifice.

¹¹ My son, do not reject or take lightly the discipline of the Lord [learn from your mistakes and the testing that comes from His correction through discipline];
Nor despise His rebuke, ¹² For those whom the Lord loves He corrects, Even as a father corrects the son in whom he delights.
Proverbs 3:11-12 (AMP)

The same Hebrew word *musar* is used in this scripture to denote that God's disciplinary correction is no different from the discipline we receive from our parents. **Ahab** is the same word defined as human love above to show us that God loves us as His children just as we love our children and want the best for them. When God instructed Abraham to offer his only son as a sacrifice and Abraham consented, that moment foreshadowed God's own willingness to offer His only son for humanity. Seeing His son suffering on the cross must have been deeply painful and He extends that compassion towards us.

Our attitude towards disciplinary correction matters a lot. I have observed that my child tends to resist disciplinary action when it is perceived as too strict. This often occurs when he does not understand the significance of his actions. He would then run into his room yelling "I hate consequences."

When we are corrected by God, it never feels good. It feels painful, sorrowful, grievous, sad. Then what is the reason for God's chastisement?

> ➢ To heal us

> ¹⁴ *if My people who are called by My name*
> *will humble themselves, and pray and seek My face,*
> *and turn from their wicked ways, then I will hear from*
> *heaven, and will forgive their sin and heal their land.*
> **2 Chronicles 7:14 (NKJV)**

In the preceding verse, God was telling Israel if you see my corrective action in your life: If I shut up the heavens so that no rain falls, or if I command locusts to devour the land, or if I send pestilence *and* plague among you. You can totally reverse it by getting on your knees, turning aside your plate and repenting from your wicked ways. He promised to hear, to forgive and to heal. Isaiah 59:2 (NKJV) says:

> ² *But your iniquities have separated you from your God;*
> *And your sins have hidden His face from you, So that He*
> *will not hear.*

We are God's people redeemed by the precious blood of Jesus, disobedience to His will can be an obstacle to having our prayers answered. Have you experienced a time when you couldn't sense God's presence? I have—usually, it was because I was either doing something I shouldn't or neglecting what I should. God is good at course correcting us when we return to Him in humility. We must let him into all the rooms in our heart, holding back nothing.

> ➤ To give us peace in the days of trouble

12 Blessed is the one you discipline, LORD, the one you teach from your law;
13 you grant them relief from days of trouble, till a pit is dug for the wicked.
Psalm 94:12-13 (NIV)

Blessed, happy is the one God corrects, chastens, the one He teaches, instructs from His word. God will not waste time correcting you if He has nothing to teach you. The end goal is to grant us relief. Relief is the Hebrew word **saqat** – to be tranquil, to be at peace, rest, lie still. Jesus said in John 16:33, in this world you will have trouble, but take heart I have overcome the world. If you submit to the discipline of the Lord, you will have rest, lie still in the days of trouble – evil, malignant, injury, calamity, hurtful days. You will not be shaken, you will be at peace.

> ➤ To acquire understanding

32 He who neglects and ignores instruction and discipline despises himself, But he who learns from rebuke acquires understanding [and grows in wisdom].
Proverbs 15:32 (AMP)

The soul flourishes when aligned with its creator. Disobedience can throw us out of alignment. If you reject discipline, you hate your own soul because you are depriving it of understanding, growth, peace, and healing. You are technically starving yourself by limiting opportunities for self-improvement. God's disciplinary approach varies depending on the individual because what works for you may not work for me.

Recently, I experienced disciplinary action due to not completing this book within the designated timeframe following the revelation of the book. As a result, it seemed as though my personal progress was temporarily halted. My personal prayers weren't answered, but those I made for others were. Even with prayer and fasting, nothing seems to change.

I listened to sermons both at church and online, and each consistently emphasized a central message: one must complete what has been started. Progress with God requires obedience, and advancement is not possible beyond one's last act of disobedience, regardless of how minor the assignment may appear. I was like, "ok God, I get it, I will sit my behind down and complete this task." I wanted to finish the book, but my full-time job and parenting responsibilities meant I could only write when I had time. Like Martha, I focused on staying occupied with daily activities, which resulted in increased busyness but yielded few tangible outcomes. I acknowledged that I procrastinated and did not prioritize this assignment as highly as I should have, I repented for it and went to work.

If we learn from rebuke, if we consent, agree, yield to the discipline of the Lord, we will possess understanding and grow in knowledge. Proverbs 4:7 tells us that wisdom is the principal thing, in all our getting to get understanding.

Whoever loves instruction and discipline loves knowledge,
But he who hates reproof and correction is stupid.
Proverbs 12:1 (AMP)

If you love discipline, you love knowledge - discernment, wisdom and understanding. Surrendering to God's discipline is totally worth it. It might not make sense in the moment, but if you give it time, you will be thankful for the rewards. It will save your soul.

4. Discipline for our flesh:

Finally, the fourth way that the word of God is profitable to us in the season of instruction in righteousness is to discipline our flesh.

*27 But [like a boxer] I strictly **discipline** my body and make it my slave, so that, after I have preached [the gospel] to others, I myself will not somehow be disqualified [as unfit for service].*
1 Corinthians 9:27 (AMP)

*Discipline here is **Hypopiazo** in Greek which is different from* **paideia** (instruction). It means keep under, subdue one's passion, <u>to beat black and blue</u>, like a boxer one buffets the body, handle it roughly, discipline by hardship.

Olympic athletes undergo rigorous training in preparation for their single day of competition, motivated by the goal of winning a gold medal. They subject themselves to intensive physical conditioning, continuously pushing their bodies to achieve peak performance. Paul in the above scripture compares himself to an athlete. You may ask, why is this powerful apostle beating himself black and blue for? I am glad you asked. Let's look at Galatians 5:21b (AMP):

I warn you beforehand, just as I did previously, that those who practice such things will not inherit the kingdom of God.

What type of practice will keep us from inheriting the kingdom of God? Living according to the flesh – Paul lists them out in Galatians 5:20-21:

they are sexual immorality, impurity, sensuality (total irresponsibility, lack of self-control), [20] idolatry, sorcery, hostility, strife, jealousy, fits of anger, disputes, dissensions, factions [that promote heresies], [21] envy, drunkenness, riotous behavior, and other things like these.

Paul is telling us that he disciplines his flesh by making his flesh a slave, he does not allow his flesh to lead. His spirit that is subject to the Holy Spirit drives the flesh. He has suffered too much for the kingdom, gone to jail, flogged, shipwrecked, faced persecutions. All his sacrifices will be counted as nothing if he was disqualified for the final prize just because he made his flesh an idol. He had too much at stake. So, Paul makes an intentional decision to align both his private and public life with the principles outlined in the word of God. He did not preach one thing and lived another way.

¹⁶ So I say, walk by the Spirit, and you will not gratify the desires of the flesh. ¹⁷ For the flesh desires what is contrary to the Spirit, and the Spirit what is contrary to the flesh. They are in conflict with each other, so that you are not to do whatever you want.
Galatians 5:16-17(NIV)

Our flesh persistently craves its own desires. Every new year, people worldwide—including myself—set resolutions. At the beginning of each year, I set a goal to maintain a healthy diet and engage in physical exercise at least three times per week. Initially, I maintain a high level of motivation when starting a gym routine.

However, by the second or third month, attending becomes progressively less engaging. Eventually, my frequency declines to once per week or only a few times per month, leading to a sense of discouragement and the decision to postpone my fitness efforts until the following year. This is insanity. Paul describes my situation best in Romans 7:18-19 (MSG):

17-20 But I need something more! For if I know the law but still can't keep it, and if the power of sin within me keeps sabotaging my best intentions, I obviously need help! I realize that I don't have what it takes. I can will it, but I can't do it. I decide to do good, but I don't really do it; I decide not to do bad, but then I do it anyway. My decisions, such as they are, don't result in actions. Something has gone wrong deep within me and gets the better of me every time.

We have all been down the road of good intentions, wanting to live right, to obey God, to walk in purity and discovered that its feels very hard to overcome the flesh and stay in the game. Do we give up and not try? Do we stay down, or do we get back up? At some point we all must make the decision to put the flesh under with the help of the Holy Spirit if we want to obtain the prize of our high calling in Christ.

The prize that Paul did not want to miss is the kingdom of God.

16 Instead, they were longing for a better country—a heavenly one. Therefore God is not ashamed to be called their God, for he has prepared a city for them.
Hebrews 11:16 (NIV)

Paul is not saying that it is easy, no sir. He was a man just like us, but living a disciplined life meant dying daily.

12-14 I'm not saying that I have this all together, that I have it made. But I am well on my way, reaching out for Christ, who has so wondrously reached out for me. Friends, don't get me wrong: By no means do I count myself an expert in all of this, but I've got my eye on the goal, where God is beckoning us onward—to Jesus. I'm off and running, and I'm not turning back.
Philippians 3:12-14 (MSG)

Paul took the baton from the moment he was called by Christ, he embraced his mission with determination and unwavering commitment, took off running, never once looking back. In his race, he ran into opposition, troubles, jail time. He persevered and kept running the race after each release from prison.

19 Pray also for me, that whenever I speak, words may be given me so that I will fearlessly make known the mystery of the gospel, 20 for which I am an ambassador in chains. Pray that I may declare it fearlessly, as I should.
Ephesians 6:19-20 (NIV)

In our struggle against sin, we have not resisted to the point of shedding our blood (Hebrew 12:4). Ask yourself what are the factors that may be hindering your personal progress? Consider ways to move forward in your commitment to Christ. Run towards the mark of your high calling. Remember Joseph, Jacob's son, Genesis 39:6 described him as well built and handsome. During his time in Potiphar's house, when Potiphar's wife tried to entice him, he ran. His run from sin landed him in jail yet he maintained course.

¹⁹ If we who are [abiding] in Christ have hoped only in this life [and this is all there is], then we are of all people most miserable and to be pitied.
1 Corinthians 15:19 (AMP)

This life is not all that there is, we have a heavenly home country waiting for us. We are surrounded by thousands upon thousands of angels and a cloud of witnesses so let's take the baton and run without looking back.

CHAPTER SIX

THE SEASON OF INSTRUCTION IN RIGHTEOUSNESS PT. 2

*"All scripture is given by inspiration of God, and is profitable for doctrine, for reproof, for correction, for **instruction** in righteousness: 17 That the man of God may be perfect, thoroughly furnished unto all good works.*

2 Timothy 3:16-17 (KJV)

How do we develop a disciplined life?

*Discipline as we saw in the preceding chapter is the Greek word **Hypopiazo** which is different from **paideia** (training, instruction). It means keep under, subdue one's passion, to beat black and blue, like a boxer one buffets the body, handle it roughly, discipline by hardship.*

27 *But [like a boxer] I strictly **discipline** my body and make it my slave, so that, after I have preached [the gospel] to others, I myself will not somehow be disqualified [as unfit for service].*
1 Corinthians 9:27(AMP)

1. We develop a disciplined life by praying always.

When I was a young child, my praying mother used to say all the time "that a Christian soldier fights best on her knees."

It happened that while Jesus was praying in a certain place, after He finished, one of His disciples said to Him, "Lord, teach us to pray just as John also taught his disciples." ² He said to them, "WhEn you pray,
Luke 11:1-2 (AMP)

Jesus said **when** you pray, not **if** you pray. Why did the disciples ask Jesus to teach them to pray? They saw the result of prayer in His life - the effectiveness of His ministry and His oneness with God. It is written that Jesus would often go away from them to pray as stated in the following scriptures:

¹² Now at this time Jesus went off to the mountain to pray, and He spent the whole night in prayer to God.
Luke 6:12 (AMP)

¹⁶ But Jesus Himself would often slip away to the wilderness and pray [in seclusion].
Luke 5:16 (AMP)

²³ After He had dismissed the crowds, He went up on the mountain by Himself to pray. When it was evening, He was there alone.
Matthew 14:23 (AMP)

*35 Early in the morning, while it was still dark, Jesus got up, left
[the house], and went out to a secluded place, and was
praying there.*
Mark 1:35(AMP)

Why did Jesus make an intentional decision to slip away and
pray? He was God in the flesh, yet he maintained daily
communication with God. He prayed in the evening, early in
the morning and through the night. Jesus also prayed and
fasted 40 days and 40 nights. I believe this was to model for
us what He taught them in Matthew 6:10:

*Your kingdom come, your will be done
On earth as it is in heaven.*
Matthew 6:10 (AMP)

In prayer, we are partnering with God to bring His will down
on earth. The devil cannot do anything through man without
his consent or agreement. God can but chooses our
partnership. Our prayer is giving God consent to establish
His will on earth as it is in heaven. We become a conduit of
heaven through prayer. This tells me that prayer is not an
option, it is a necessity, it is our lifeline. We cannot simply
wake up and commence our day without spending
intentional time in prayer. We organize our day through
prayer, without prayer we will be powerless. Without prayer
we will be like fish out of water, we would die spiritually
without our daily charge. A prayerless Christian is a
powerless Christian.

The heartfelt and persistent prayer of a righteous man (believer) can accomplish much [when put into action and made effective by God—it is dynamic and can have tremendous power]
James 5:16b (AMP)

Through prayer we contend for your faith. Contend means to fight, to challenge, to struggle, to battle, to wrestle. When God told Joshua that He has given Jericho into his hands, I thought it was a done deal, Joshua still had to lead Israel into battle and follow God's strategy to conquer the city.

² The Lord said to Joshua, "See, I have given Jericho into your hand, with its king and the mighty warriors. ³ Now you shall march around the city, all the men of war circling the city once. You shall do this [once each day] for six days.
Joshua 6:2-3 (AMP)

Joshua believed God and went to war. He and all of Isreal obeyed the directive given to them and conquered Jericho. God spoke and they marched. The victory starts with the word. We all want God to speak to us but remember that when He speaks the victory is guaranteed but we must fight for it, we must contend for the promise.

♦ *When God gives you a word, a promise, you will have to contend for it on your knees.*

God told Elijah to tell Ahab that it was going to rain,

After a long time, in the third year, the word of the Lord came to Elijah: "Go and present yourself to Ahab, and I will send rain on the land."
1 Kings 18:1 (NIV)

God said He would send rain and yet there was no rain and no sign of rain.

⁴¹ And Elijah said to Ahab, "Go, eat and drink, for there is the sound of a heavy rain."
1 Kings 18:41 (NIV)

Only Elijah could hear that sound, because when he said it there were no clouds to be seen in the sky. It still looked dry in the physical. Ahab believed the word of God spoken through Elijah and went off to eat, Elijah went off to pray.

⁴² So Ahab went off to eat and drink, but Elijah climbed to the top of Carmel, bent down to the ground and put his face between his knees. ⁴³ "Go and look toward the sea," he told his servant. And he went up and looked. "There is nothing there," he said. **_Seven times_** *Elijah said, "Go back."*

⁴⁴ The seventh time the servant reported, "A cloud as small as a man's hand is rising from the sea." So Elijah said, "Go and tell Ahab, 'Hitch up your chariot and go down before the rain stops you.

45 Meanwhile, the sky grew black with clouds, the wind rose, a heavy rain started falling and Ahab rode off to Jezreel. 46 The power of the Lord came on Elijah and, tucking his cloak into his belt, he ran ahead of Ahab all the way to Jezreel.
1 Kings 18:42-46 (NIV)

God promised rain BUT why did Elijah have to stay on his knees till rain fell? Elijah stayed on his knees till there was a cloud formation. This is an example of the manifestation of God's will on earth as it is in heaven with man's participation. James 5:17-18 (AMP) sums it up:

17 Elijah was a man with a nature like ours [with the same physical, mental, and spiritual limitations and shortcomings], and he prayed intensely for it not to rain, and it did not rain on the earth for three years and six months. 18 Then he prayed again, and the sky gave rain and the land produced its crops [as usual].

I have been guilty of doing what Ahab did. I may receive a prophetic word –

via a dream:

For God does speak—now one way, now another - though no one perceives it. 15 In a dream, in a vision of the night, when deep sleep falls on people as they slumber in their beds, 16 he may speak in their ears and terrify them with warnings,

¹⁷ to turn them from wrongdoing and keep them from pride,
¹⁸ to preserve them from the pit,
their lives from perishing by the sword.
Job 33: 14-18 (NIV)

via His written word:

¹⁷ So then faith comes by hearing, and hearing by the word of God.
Romans 10:17 (NKJV)

via His Holy Spirit:

¹³ But when he, the Spirit of truth, comes, he will guide you into all the truth. He will not speak on his own; he will speak only what he hears, and he will tell you what is yet to come.
John 16:13 (NIV)

via the still small voice:

¹² and after the earthquake a fire, but the Lord was not in the fire; and after the fire a still small voice. ¹³ So it was, when Elijah heard it, that he wrapped his face in his mantle and went out and stood in the entrance of the cave. Suddenly a voice came to him, and said, "What are you doing here, Elijah?"
1 Kings 19:12-15 (NKJV)

---

or via a preaching or prophecy,

I shout about it, I write it down, I share it with friends, "won't He do it" and just like Ahab I go back to my activities of daily living – eating, drinking, lifeing while waiting for God to perform what He said. But Elijah got on his knees and did not rise till he had birthed the spoken word.

What is it that these men of old understood that our generation is still grappling with? They did not seek to fulfil their own desires in prayer; rather, they sought to align with God's will. We seek Him to know what His will is regarding a matter and then we posture our heart to pray for what He reveals.

Let's look at David, a man after God's own heart. We touched on inquiring of God a couple pages above but let's dig deeper. Before going to battle David would inquire of the Lord for direction. To inquire is to ask, pray, consult, enquire carefully, ask counsel. In 1 Samuel 30, David and his men returned from battle to discover that the enemy had raided their camp and captured their women and children. The bible says they wept until they had no more strength to weep. David's men were so distressed by it that they spoke of stoning David.

⁸ David inquired of the Lord, saying, "Shall I pursue this band [of raiders]? Will I overtake them?" And He answered him, "Pursue, for you will certainly overtake them, and you will certainly rescue [the captives]." ⁹ So David went, he and the six hundred men who were with him, and came to the brook

Besor; there those [who could not continue] remained behind.
1Samuel 30:8-9 (AMP)

David went in to God in prayer. He knew he should pursue his enemies who had taken his family captive. That is a no brainer, but he humbled himself to ask God what He should do. It reminds me of when Moses told God that they would not go without His presence, we can but we don't want to,

"How will anyone know that you are pleased with me and with your people unless you go with us? What else will distinguish me and your people from all the other people on the face of the earth?"
Exodus 33:16 (NIV)

The presence of God sets us apart and there is no victory without His glory. Moses knew it and David knew it too. David was not willing to engage in a battle that God did not sanction. He had seen God use him to take down a giant in battle with just one smooth stone.

[17] Then David [and his men] struck them down [in battle] from twilight until the evening of the next day; and not a man of them escaped, except four hundred young men who rode camels and fled. [18] So David recovered all that the Amalekites had taken and rescued his two wives. [19] Nothing of theirs was missing whether small or great, sons or daughters, spoil or anything that had been taken; David recovered it all.
1Samuel 30:17-19 (AMP)

David recovered all, he knew victory was guaranteed when he aligned himself with the Lord. This became a common practice in David's life; it was his lifestyle. When He slayed Goliath, he fought and slayed Goliath in the name of the Lord of Hosts, Jehovah Sabaoth. Right after David was made king, the Philistines came against him in battle in 2 Samuel 5:19-20, it says:

19 David <u>inquired</u> of the Lord, saying, "Shall I go up against the Philistines? Will You hand them over to me?" And the Lord said to David, "Go up, for I will certainly hand them over to you." 20 So David came to Baal-perazim, and he defeated them there, and said, "The Lord has broken through my enemies before me, like a breakthrough of water." So he named that place Baal-perazim (master of breakthroughs).
2 Samuel 5:19-20 (AMP)

David recognized and acknowledged God as the Lord of breakthroughs. Do you need a breakthrough in a particular area of your life? The master of breakthroughs is just a prayer away.

The Philistines once more engaged David in a battle Given that it was the same adversary, one might assume that having previously defeated them would indicate it is appropriate and might even be God's will for him to engage in battle again, following the earlier strategy. David, however, humbled himself and sought guidance from God, who provided a new battle plan.

²² Once more the Philistines came up and spread out in the Valley of Rephaim; ²³ so David inquired of the Lord, and he answered, "Do not go straight up, but circle around behind them and attack them in front of the poplar trees. ²⁴ As soon as you hear the sound of marching in the tops of the poplar trees, move quickly, because that will mean the Lord has gone out in front of you to strike the Philistine army." ²⁵ So David did as the Lord commanded him, and he struck down the Philistines all the way from Gibeon to Gezer.
2 Samuel 5: 22-25 (NIV)

Although facing the same adversary, a different battle strategy was employed. In the first battle, David went ahead and conquered his enemies. In the second battle God marched in front and started the attack, David joined in and won the battle. Maybe David learnt this from Joshua's mistake with the people Gibeon. On the way to the promised land, God had commanded the Israelites to destroy all the land's inhabitants before them. Men from Gibeon deceived Isreal into making an agreement with them to let them live by pretending they were from a faraway country.

¹⁴ The Israelites sampled their provisions but did not inquire of the Lord. ¹⁵ Then Joshua made a treaty of peace with them to let them live, and the leaders of the assembly ratified it by oath.¹⁶ Three days after they made the treaty with the Gibeonites, the Israelites heard that they were neighbors, living near them. ¹⁷ So the Israelites set out and on the third day came to their cities: Gibeon, Kephirah, Beeroth and Kiriath Jearim. ¹⁸ But the Israelites did not attack them, because the leaders of the assembly had sworn an

oath to them by the Lord, the God of Israel. The whole
assembly grumbled against the leaders
Joshua 9:14-18 (NIV)

The Israelites entered a treaty of peace with the Gibeonites without consulting God. Why seek God's counsel? Because man's heart is deceptively wicked only God knows it. We often make major life-altering decisions without dedicating time to prayer and seeking divine guidance regarding the plan, strategy, and anticipated outcome. Jesus spent forty days and forty nights fasting prior to calling the disciples. We tend to choose the familiar path rather than take the well tested road of prayer. Rather than simply presenting requests to God, we should seek His guidance to gain insight into the situation, discern appropriate actions, and determine the best approach.

Psalm 34:10 (NKJV) says,

[10] The young lions lack and suffer hunger;
But those who seek the Lord shall not lack any good thing.

To seek is the Hebrew word ***daras*** meaning to enquire, require, inquire. There is no want, lack, need, poverty to those who seek God. This suggests that we should shift our focus from presenting our personal needs and desires, but instead seek to understand God's will, intentions or guidance for the day. We then intercede for the revelation we receive from him. Prayer is warfare because the enemy is not going to sit idle or fold his hands and watch us take territories that Adam gave him legally. That is why Jesus came and died for us. Jesus came, died and give us the tools for our warfare:

- He gave us His name which is above every name proving He has absolute power, unlimited authority, answers to no one and has jurisdiction over everything.
- He sent us the Holy Ghost as our Helper (Comforter, Advocate, Intercessor—Counselor, Strengthener, Standby) who helps us in or weakness by interceding for us in accordance with God's will.
- He gave us His blood which speaks a better word than the blood of Abel by crying mercy on our behalf.
- He gave us His word which according to Jeremiah 23:29 (AMP) is like a hammer that breaks the [most stubborn] rock (stronghold) in pieces.
- He gave us the authority (right) and power (ability) to cast out unclean spirits and to heal all kinds of diseases.
- He gave us the keys (authority) of the kingdom of heaven, and whatever we forbid on earth will be forbidden in heaven, and whatever we permit on earth will be allowed in heaven.
- He also taught us how to pray, which according to Philippians 4:6 is a huge key to overcoming worry and anxiety. The good news is that God hears us when we pray, He is never too busy for us.
    14 Now this is the confidence that we have in Him, that if we ask anything according to His will, He hears us. 15 And if we know that He hears us,

whatever we ask, we know that we have the petitions
that we have asked of Him.
1 John 5:14-15(NKJV)

- He gave us His full armor which according to Ephesians 6:11 enables us to stand against the devil's schemes.
- He gave us the angels who do the bidding of the word of God that we speak.

[20] Bless the Lord, you His angels, you mighty ones who do His
commandments,
Obeying the voice of His word!
Psalm 103:20 (AMP)

Angels obey the voice – the Hebrew word **qol** meaning sound, voice, proclamation, cry, noise of the word of God. The words we speak are powerful. There are literally mighty warriors who are positioned to obey the word of God we speak. If you give voice to His word, the angels will obey it. Hebrews 1:14 says,

[14] Are not all the angels ministering spirits <u>sent out</u> [by God] to
serve (accompany, protect) those who will inherit salvation?
[Of course they are!]
Hebrews 1:14 (AMP)

Apostello is the Greek word for sent out meaning to order one to go to a place appointed, to send out on a mission. We inherited salvation when we accepted Jesus as Lord.

Immediately we were assigned angels to minister, serve, accompany, protect, provide relief to us but we must speak the word of God. They obey the voice of His word.

> [11] For He will command His angels in regard to you,
> To protect and defend and guard you in all your ways [of obedience and service].
> **Psalm 91:11**

The command has been given to angels; our job is to release the word.

2. *We develop a disciplined life by studying and meditating on the word of God.*

When we pray, we are essentially asking for God's will to be done on earth as it is in heaven. How then can we pray without a knowledge of God's will? His will is made known to us through His word. David in Psalm 40:8 (AMP) said,

> [8] "I delight to do Your will, O my God; Your law is within my heart."

May-aw is the Hebrew word for within meaning inward parts, bowels, belly, heart, womb. To follow God's will (pleasure, desire), David placed God's law in the middle of his inward parts.

Meditating on the word of God is a way to store up the word in our inmost part so we can pull from it in times of trouble. Thank God for the Holy Ghost who also helps to remind us of the word.

God told Jeremiah in chapter 1 verse 12 (NKJV):

> [12] *Then the Lord said to me, "You have seen well, for I am ready to <u>perform</u> My word."*

Asa is the Hebrew word for perform meaning to work, execute, accomplish, make, perform. This is the same word for accomplish used in Isaiah 55:11 (NKJV):

> [11] *So shall My word be that goes forth from My mouth; It shall not return to Me void,*
> *But it shall <u>accomplish</u> **(Asa)** what I please,*
> *And it shall prosper in the thing for which I sent it.*

When we do our part - study the word, meditate on the word, take it in just like when we take our medications, speak it, believe it and obey it, God does His part. His part is to work the word – He performs His word, He accomplishes His word.

> [24] This *is* the day the Lord has <u>made</u> *(Asa);* We will rejoice and be glad in it.
> **Psalm 118:24**

Asa is the Hebrew word for made. Each day that we wake up is a day that God is looking to execute His word – the building block of our life. What will we give Him to work with, His words or complaints? Our input when we wake up will determine the outcome of the day – if we are going to rejoice and be glad. We are part of a speaking kingdom. God said let there be and it became. Speak, do not remain silent. When you wake up in the morning declare "this is the day the Lord has made all things to work together for my good, He has made everything I touch to prosper according to His word, so I will rejoice and be glad."

The angels of the Lord do the bidding of God's word. You say it, they run with it. All of nature is waiting for the revealing of the sons of God, for us to disclose the truth of His word.

Ephesians 6:17 mentions the word of God as one of the armors of God.

17b and the sword of the Spirit, which is the Word of God.

The word of God is the sword of the Spirit. It is the only armor that is a weapon of offence. It is sharper than any double-edged sword:

12 For the word of God is living and active and full of power [making it operative, energizing, and effective]. It is sharper than any two-edged sword, penetrating as far as the division of the soul and spirit [the completeness of a person], and of both joints and marrow [the deepest parts of our nature], exposing and judging the very thoughts and intentions of the heart.
Hebrews 4:12 (AMP)

How do we wage war with the word of God? We demolish strongholds with the word:

29 "Is not My word like fire [that consumes all that cannot endure the test]?" says the Lord, "and like a hammer that breaks the [most stubborn] rock [in pieces]?
Jeremiah 23:29 (AMP)

The word rock is the Hebrew word **sela**, one of its meanings is stronghold. We can use the word of God like a hammer to break strongholds. 2 Corinthians 10:4 tells us that the weapons of our warfare are not carnal (they are not the weapons of this world) but mighty through God to the pulling down of strongholds. We use our sword weapon which works like a hammer to demolish the strongholds in our lives.

On God's word rests our faith, it is our daily bread that gives us the power to overcome the enemy. It is through the word of God that we can overcome temptation. Jesus, guided by the Spirit into the wilderness, successfully resisted the devil by relying on the authority of the word of God. Jesus, referred to in scripture as "the Word made flesh," used God's word to overcome the enemy—how much more do we need to study, know, and use God's word in our own lives.

11 And they have overcome (conquered) him by means of the blood of the Lamb and by the utterance of their testimony,

for they did not love and cling to life even when faced with death [holding their lives cheap till they had to die for their witnessing].
Revelation 12:11 (AMPC)

Nikao is the Greek word for overcome meaning to win the case, maintain one's cause, to subdue, conquer, overcome, prevail. They subdued, won the case against the enemy by the blood of the lamb and by the utterance – Greek word **logos** meaning the sayings of God, word of God, Christ - account, cause, communication, preaching. We know that according to John 1:1 in the beginning was the word (logos), and the word (logos) was with God, and the word (logos) was God.

Even when faced with death, they uttered the word of God, they defeated the enemy by speaking, witnessing, testifying the word of God because they knew that this earthy life is not the prize. By now we should be familiar with this scripture I keep quoting, "if for this life alone we have hope in Christ, we are of all men most miserable (1 Corinthians 15:19)." Our victory does not only come in the form of earthly conquests.

3. *We develop a disciplined life by appropriating the power of the blood.*

[13] *The blood shall be a sign for you on [the doorposts of] the houses where you live; when I see the blood I shall pass over you, and no affliction shall happen to you to destroy you when I strike the land of Egypt.*
Exodus 12:13 (AMP)

When I see the blood – Hebrew word **dam** meaning bloodshed, I will pass over you. It does not say when I see you, my people I will pass over you. The LORD was looking for blood on door frames which represented bloodshed – death has already occurred in this house, let's move on. If an Israelite first-born male had been present as a guest in the home of an Egyptian acquaintance on that night, would he have been spared? Not unless there's blood on the door. This would result in death by association. Would an Egyptian first-born male visiting an Israelite that night have survived? Probably, if the Israelite family followed instructions and applied blood to the door frame of their house.

The blood of an animal was used to seal the old covenant as stated in Exodus 24:8 (NIV),

[8] Moses then took the blood, sprinkled it on the people and said, "This is the blood of the covenant that the Lord has made with you in accordance with all these words."

If you confess with your mouth that Jesus is Lord and believe with your heart that God raised Him from the dead, you shall be saved (Romans 10:9). This is the prayer of salvation, if you accept Jesus and make Him Lord over your life it brings you into a new covenant (agreement) with God.

15 For this reason He is the Mediator and Negotiator of a new covenant [that is, an entirely new agreement uniting God and man], so that those who have been called [by God] may receive [the fulfillment of] the promised eternal inheritance, since a death has taken place [as the payment] which redeems them from the sins committed under the obsolete first covenant.
Hebrews 9:15 (AMP)

This new covenant with God is sealed with the blood of Jesus signifying that death has taken place and payment has been made in full, no partial payments in this kingdom.

28 for this is My blood of the [new and better] covenant, which [ratifies the agreement and] is being poured out for many [as a substitutionary atonement] for the forgiveness of sins.
Matthew 26:28 (AMP)

Haima the Greek word for blood of man or animal refers to the seat of life. Life of Jesus is in His blood. We are forgiven, redeemed, delivered, healed, justified, preserved, saved, and protected by His blood. This is what the blood of Jesus paid for and so much more.

22 In fact under the Law almost everything is cleansed with blood, and without the shedding of blood there is no forgiveness [neither release from sin and its guilt, nor cancellation of the merited punishment].
Hebrews 9:22 (AMP)

By the blood we are not only forgiven but we are also released from the punishment that our sins deserved, we are released from death. The blood signifies that death has taken place here and the payment has been made in full. We need to appropriate the blood of Jesus. Appropriation sounds like a big word – it means take (something) for one's own use, typically without the owner's permission. Its synonyms include seize, commandeer, take possession of, take over, assume, hijack. Look the devil in the eye and say,

"By the blood of Jesus I am forgiven, redeemed, justified, healed, delivered, protected, saved, blessed and released from the punishment - curse, sickness, destruction, and death that my sins deserved – death has taken place here and the payment has been made in full. Thank you Lord for your sacrifice."

[11] *And they have overcome (conquered) him by means of the blood of the Lamb*
Revelation 12:11a (AMP)

We overcome, conquer, subdue, win the case by the blood of Jesus. This is the blood that speaks better things.

[24] *and to Jesus, the Mediator of a new covenant [uniting God and man], and to the sprinkled blood, which speaks [of mercy], a better and nobler and more gracious message than the blood of Abel [which cried out for vengeance].*
Hebrews 12:24 (AMP)

Jesus is the negotiator of the new covenant. When he came to broker peace and to restore friendship with God, He was crucified. His blood cried out for mercy not vengeance and still speaks mercy. By the blood of Jesus we overcome him – the accuser of the brethren, who accuses us day and night before our God (Revelation 12:10b). Our accuser is furious and relentless because his time is short, but we have the blood of Jesus, and we can appropriate it to win the case.

The blood of Jesus speaks a better word than the blood of Abel. The blood of Abel cried for vengeance, but the blood of Jesus speaks mercy and silences every other voice speaking or crying against us.

4. We develop a disciplined life by living a fasted life.

Fasting the bible way helps us subdue or discipline our flesh. The bible way of fasting is to abstain from food for a time to pray and seek God's face. When we fast the bible way, we are denying the flesh it's desires. It is a way of humbling ourselves before God.

[16] "When you fast, do not look somber as the hypocrites do, for they disfigure their faces to show others they are fasting. Truly I tell you, they have received their reward in full. [17] But when you fast, put oil on your head and wash your face, [18] so that it will not be obvious to others that you are fasting, but only to your Father, who is unseen; and your Father, who sees what is done in secret, will reward you.
Matthew 6:16-18 (NIV)

When Jesus was on earth, though being God did not see equality with God something to be used to His own advantage (Philippians 2:6). He humbled himself and fasted forty days and forty nights. He overcame temptation in the wilderness and chose the twelve disciples after this fast. He said here **when** we fast, not **if** we fast. When is the Greek word ***hotan,*** meaning as long as, as soon as. As long as you fast, as soon as you fast – fasting like prayer should be a lifestyle.

We shouldn't pray only in times of trouble; prayer is a daily practice that brings us closer to God. The bible says we should pray without ceasing, the more we pray the stronger our prayer muscles become. Fasting should also be approached this way. I have realized that I tend to fast only when confronted with challenges. But Fasting ought to be a routine. It is advisable to adopt fasting as a habit, and to engage in it particularly before making significant life decisions.

21 There, by the Ahava Canal, I proclaimed a fast, so that we might humble ourselves before our God and ask him for a safe journey for us and our children, with all our possessions. 22 I was ashamed to ask the king for soldiers and horsemen to protect us from enemies on the road, because we had told the king, "The gracious hand of our God is on everyone who looks to him, but his great anger is against all who forsake him." 23 So we fasted and petitioned our God about this, and he answered our prayer.
Ezra 8:21-23(NIV)

Ezra was traveling from Babylon to Jerusalem, a journey that would take four months. He was going to Jerusalem to teach the exiles who had returned to Israel from Babylon the law of the Lord. He was a descendant of Aaron, the chief priest. Ezra 7:6 &10 (AMP) describes Ezra as:

6 this Ezra went up from Babylon. He was a scribe skilled in the Law (the five books) of Moses, which the Lord God of Israel had given; and the king granted him everything that he asked, for the hand of the Lord his God was on him.

10 For Ezra had set his heart (resolved) to study and interpret the Law of the Lord, and to practice it and teach His statutes and ordinances in Israel.

Ezra did not just study the law, he practiced it, and he was willing to risk his life to teach the law to the exiles who have been away from Jerusalem for a very long time. The hand of God was on Ezra and the almost two thousand men he was travelling with, women and children were not included in this number. Ezra was confident in his speech to the King that God would be with them, but he did not take it for granted. They could have prayed a blessing on the multitude and called it a day. But he knew that to guarantee safe passage for all the people that were with him that they needed to fast and seek God for protection. They humbled themselves and God answered them. Fasting humbles us, when we bring ourselves low, we see God mighty and highly lifted up.

⁶ Therefore humble yourselves under the mighty hand of God [set aside self-righteous pride], so that He may exalt you [to a place of honor in His service] at the appropriate time,
1 Peter 5:6 (AMP)

Kairos is the Greek word for appropriate time meaning a fixed and definite time, the time when things are brought to crisis, opportune or seasonable time. When we humble ourselves to seek God's face He elevates us in our season of crisis.

A habit of praying and fasting is an act of worship to our God. The call of God on Paul and Barnabas was revealed by the Holy Spirit while they were doing their routine prayer and fasting.

² While they were worshiping the Lord and fasting, the Holy Spirit said, "Set apart for me Barnabas and Saul for the work to which I have called them."
Acts 13:2 (NIV)

It marked the beginning of Paul's initial missionary journeys, which opened the door to the evangelization of the Gentiles, providing them an opportunity to embrace the faith.

Fasting can help us overcome challenging situations by building our faith. When Jesus delivered the boy possessed by a demon, He said to His disciples that this kind can only come out by prayer and fasting.

¹⁹ Then the disciples came to Jesus privately and asked, "Why could we not drive it out?" ²⁰ He answered, "Because of your little faith [your lack of trust and confidence in the power of God]; for I assure you and most solemnly say to you, if you have [living] faith the size of a mustard seed, you will say to this mountain, 'Move from here to there,' and [if it is God's will] it will move; and nothing will be impossible for you. ²¹ [But this kind of demon does not go out except by prayer and fasting.]"
Matthew 17:19-21 (AMP)

The boy had been possessed by a demon that had robbed him of speech since he was a child. The moment the demon came out, the boy was healed. His healing was tied to his deliverance suggesting that sometimes deliverance precedes healing. The disciples when they inquired of the Lord the reason why they could not drive it out, Jesus said "this kind of demon does not come out except by prayer and fasting."

I appreciate that they asked the Lord why they couldn't do as He instructed. He had given them authority (right) and power (ability) to cast out unclean spirits and to heal diseases. How come they could not drive this clean spirit out? Sometimes when our prayers go unanswered, we often assume it is not God's will and shift our focus to other requests. We do not take time to ask- inquire from God why, to find out if there was something we could have done differently. Did we pray amiss? Did we seek His will before we went all in? We miss the opportunity to learn and to grow. A question like, "Lord why could we not drive it out?", can endear us to God because it is asked from a teachable heart.

My son sometimes will ask me, "mom why did you not buy me the Roblox I wanted for my birthday, is it because I am spending too much time on games or do you not have the money?" His inquiry typically fosters constructive dialogue and facilitates mutual understanding. As a parent, I appreciate his willingness to seek feedback after experiencing disappointment when he did not receive what he wanted. His humility and desire to understand how he could improve or earn the opportunity in the future foster a stronger connection between us during such moments.

Jesus said, "this kind" – the Greek word **genos** meaning kindred, offspring, generation, family. This kind of demon was rooted in the blood line. What negative pattern repeats in your family? A man shared with me that his grandfather, father, and brother all died of heart attacks. He was experiencing chest pain and feared he might suffer the same fate. I do not need a prophet to tell me that this was rooted in his blood line.

After my divorce was finalized, I suddenly began to take notice of a pattern of broken marriages in my family on my mother's side. My mom was divorced prior to marrying my dad, two of my siblings were divorced before me. Four of my mom's siblings were divorced and some of my cousins as well. Upon further investigation, I observed not only a trend of divorces, but late marriages, marital abandonment, rejection, incest and molestation among nearly all my grandmother's children, rather than a pattern of long-lasting marriages.

Since my grandmother was deceased, I consulted my mother to learn more about the relationship between my grandparents. She informed me that her father, my grandfather, had children from an earlier marriage before marrying my grandmother. His prior marriage was marked by significant challenges, and his children from that relationship were engaged in occult practices. He got saved and entered the ministry as a pastor before marrying my grandmother. Before his death, he and my grandmother had six children together, with my mother being the eldest. Following my grandfather's passing, his family arranged for my grandmother to marry her stepson, who was my grandfather's son from his previous marriage and he was involved in the occult. This happened in West Africa. The reason they gave for this abomination was that it was the culture back then, that she was a young widow with young children and they did not want her to return to her father's house, they wanted to keep her and her children in the family home. My grandmother became her stepson's wife and bore two children for him. My mom recalls that when my grandmother will go off to work (she traded food items in the local market), her new husband will try to molest my mother and her sister who where his stepsisters. He was both their stepbrother, stepdad, and molester.

My mom's story opened my eyes to see the generational curse at work in the bloodline because a recurring pattern of marital issues, incest's and molestation appears to be affecting my grandmother's children. Five family members that I know of were molested as children, four out of the five were molested by very close family members. These represent only a select number of individuals who chose to share their experiences.

A recurring negative pattern is an indication that there is an underlying curse at work. Where there is a curse, there is often an evil covenant. An evil covenant or agreement is a binding promise, pact, or contract that comes with rules and obligations—sometimes formed intentionally through rituals, oaths, or specific actions, and other times entered into unknowingly. It results in negative consequences for future generations. Consent for these covenants is often obtained through obedience, be it in words or actions. The evil covenant gives familiar spirits legal ground or access to a family's bloodline to operate thereby enforcing the consequences of the curse. In this way, the curse, the covenant, and the familiar spirit are interconnected: the covenant establishes the agreement, the familiar spirit ensures its enforcement of the agreement, and the curse is the resulting negative outcome experienced by individuals or families.

How did the sin of incest bring a curse into the family? Let us examine a couple of scriptures that deal with this issue. In the New Testament, Paul's judgment on incest in the church was to hand the offender to Satan.

It is actually reported that there is sexual immorality among you, and of a kind that even pagans do not tolerate: A man is sleeping with his father's wife. ² And you are proud! Shouldn't you rather have gone into mourning and have put out of your fellowship the man who has been doing this? ³ For my part, even though I am not physically present, I am with you in spirit. As one who is present with you in this way, I have already passed judgment in the name of our Lord Jesus on the one who has been doing this. ⁴ So when you are assembled and I am with you in spirit, and the power of our Lord Jesus is present, ⁵ hand this man over to Satan for the destruction of the flesh, so that his spirit may be saved on the day of the Lord.

1 Corinthians 5:1-5 (NIV)

In the Old Testament, the sin of incest was addressed in the following scriptures:

²⁰ "Cursed is anyone who sleeps with his father's wife, for he dishonors his father's bed." Then all the people shall say, "Amen!"

Deuteronomy 27:20 (NIV)

¹¹ The man who lies [intimately] with his father's wife has uncovered his father's nakedness; both of them shall most certainly be put to death; their blood is on them.

Leviticus 20:11(AMP)

³⁰ A man is not to marry his father's wife; he must not dishonor his father's bed.

Deuteronomy 22:30(NIV)

⁷ "'Do not dishonor your father by having sexual relations with your mother. She is your mother; do not have relations with her. ⁸ "'Do not have sexual relations with your father's

wife; that would dishonor your father.
Leviticus 18:7-8 (NIV)

The sin of incest is not a light thing. When a man sleeps with his father's wife, he brings dishonor (shame) to his father's bed and uncovers his father's nakedness. The Hebrew word to uncover is **gala** and one of its meanings is to go into exile (captives being usually stripped), captivity, reveal, shamelessly shew.

It Is not a coincidence that my grandmother's children were all held captive by the enemy through this undenounced sin.

Reuben (Jacob's firstborn) forfeited the double portion blessing of the firstborn because he slept with his father's concubine.

[22] While Israel was living in that region, Reuben went in and slept with his father's concubine Bilhah, and Israel heard of it.
Genesis 35:22 (NIV)

Jacob placed a curse on Reuben on his dying bed.

[3] "Reuben, you are my firstborn; My might, the beginning of my strength and vigor,
Preeminent in dignity and preeminent in power [that should have been your birthright].
[4] "But unstable and reckless and boiling over like water [in sinful lust], you shall not excel or have the preeminence [of the firstborn],Because you went up to your father's bed [with

Bilhah];
You defiled it—he went up to my couch.
Genesis 49:3-4 (AMP)

Reuben dishonored his father by so doing he and his descendants forfeited the blessing of the firstborn and received a curse of instability. What is the blessing of the firstborn?

¹⁷ But he shall acknowledge the son of the disliked as the firstborn by giving him <u>a double portion of all that he has</u>, for he was the first issue of his strength; the right of the firstborn is his.
Deuteronomy 21:17

The firstborn is entitled to a double portion of the inheritance.

The sons of Reuben the firstborn of Israel (he was the firstborn, but when he defiled his father's marriage bed, his rights as firstborn were given to the sons of Joseph son of Israel; so he could not be listed in the genealogical record in accordance with his birthright, ² and though Judah was the strongest of his brothers and a ruler came from him, the rights of the firstborn belonged to Joseph)—
1 Chronicles 5:1-2 (NIV)

The opposite of blessing is a curse The curse of instability was upon Reuben's bloodline. The curse continued long after Reuben was gone. Jacob pronounced the curse on Reuben on his death bed. On Moses death bed, he pronounced a blessing on Reuben reversing the curse.

"Let Reuben live and not die, nor his people be few."
Deuteronomy 33:6 (NIV)

Generational curses can be broken by breaking the evil covenant or agreement that gave the familiar spirit access. Just as an evil covenant can create a generational curse, a righteous covenant with God leads to generational blessings. The presence of a consistent positive trend within a family lineage may suggest the existence of an underlying blessing at work. The covenant established between God and Abraham provided a legal basis for God to act within Abraham's lineage and bestow blessings upon his descendants. Generational blessing became the result of that covenant as seen in Genesis 17.

[7] I will establish my covenant as an everlasting covenant between me and you and your descendants after you for the generations to come, to be your God and the God of your descendants after you. [8] The whole land of Canaan, where you now reside as a foreigner, I will give as an everlasting possession to you and your descendants after you; and I will be their God."

[9] Then God said to Abraham, "As for you, you must keep my covenant, you and your descendants after you for the generations to come. [10] This is my covenant with you and your descendants after you, the covenant you are to keep: Every male among you shall be circumcised. [11] You are to undergo circumcision, and it will be the sign of the covenant between me and you.
Genesis 17:7-11(NIV)

The descendants of Abraham were not consulted or given the opportunity to participate in the decision-making process. The moment Abraham cut that covenant with God, it became binding on his bloodline. Fortunately for them they entered into a covenant that came with a blessing. They would be in default of the covenant God made with Abraham if they refused to be circumcised because rejecting circumcision would mean failing to uphold the covenant God established with Abraham, as circumcision was a central requirement of that agreement.

In the context of this covenant, circumcision served as a physical sign of belonging to God, it demonstrated obedience to God's command, marking a lasting bond between Abraham, his descendants, and God.

[14] *Any uncircumcised male, who has not been circumcised in the flesh, will be cut off from his people; he has broken my covenant."*
Genesis 17:14 (NIV)

Considering the preceding discussion, it is clear that every covenant has a designated enforcer. Your absence or the fact that you were not born at the time the covenant was made does not preclude the enforcer from pursuing action against you. When an individual passes away with outstanding debts, those debts are not immediately canceled. Instead, payment is made from the assets of the estate of the deceased. If an estate's assets do not fully satisfy outstanding debts, debt collectors may reach out to surviving family members in an attempt to recover the remaining amounts owed. If the surviving family members did not cosign the debt, it is not legal for them to be held responsible for the debts; however, creditors may still attempt to collect because a debtor's death does not eliminate the existing debt.

If the family members are unfamiliar with applicable legal regulations, they may inadvertently settle debts owed by a deceased person. Similarly, the passing of a covenant's initiator does not invalidate the covenant; unless formally revoked, its obligations remain enforceable upon the descendants.

The devil is very legalistic, we need to be versed in the word of God to know how to defeat him with the work that Jesus did on the cross.

Marriage is a covenant. A generational curse entered the family line through a problematic marital covenant formed between a stepmother and her stepson—a relationship that allowed the spirit of incest to gain a legal foothold within the bloodline which he used to spew out his curses resulting in ongoing harmful patterns within the family, affecting relationships and well-being for generations.

This kind – **genos** goeth only by prayer and fasting. You break generational curses by breaking the evil covenant which then disarms the enforcer or familiar spirit. Neglecting to do this allows the familiar spirit in the bloodline to lie dormant waiting for an opportune time to manifest, waiting for someone to give him access. It can skip generations and manifest in the next because the evil covenant that gave it legal access has not been broken.

For instance, if I see the curse at work, and I spend time in prayer and fasting to renounce and break the curse. What I have merely done was close the access door to my own life. The familiar spirit might decide to lay dormant for a while and not bother me. But if the next generation after me are not strong in prayer or are not living for God, the access door will be reopened for those negative cycles to repeat because the legal ground has not been dealt with.

Why not deal with the root of the problem which in this case is the evil covenant? By dealing with the covenant itself—not just the symptoms/curses or the fruits—you can help ensure that future generations are free from these negative cycles.

The devil is constantly seeking an access door into our lives. 1 Peter 5:8 warns us to:

8 Be sober [well balanced and self-disciplined], be alert and cautious at all times. That enemy of yours, the devil, prowls around like a roaring lion [fiercely hungry], seeking someone to devour.
1 Peter 5:8

He is looking for an opportunity to destroy us if we give him access. After Jesus temptation in the wilderness, it is written in Luke 4:13 (NIV) that the devil left Him for an opportune time.

13 When the devil had finished all this tempting, he left him until an opportune time.

Kairos is the Greek word for opportune time which means due time, a fixed, definite time, <u>the time when things are brought to crisis</u>.

When did that opportune time manifest? The moment when the "opportune time" finally arrived was marked by Judas allowing sin to give Satan a foothold in his life. Satan had relentlessly searched for an entry point to disrupt the work of salvation. He began by presenting temptations to Jesus following His period of fasting for forty days and forty nights, during which He experienced hunger.

Unable to find any weakness in Jesus Himself, Satan turned his attention to those close to Him who were familiar with Him, searching for someone whose vulnerabilities could be exploited. As he searched, His gaze settled on two of Jesus's disciples: Peter to deny Jesus and Judas to betray Him. One way or the other one of them he planned would help further his agenda. Peter would later deny Jesus out of fear, but it was Judas who ultimately became the instrument of betrayal, exchanging his loyalty for thirty pieces of silver, he sealed the agreement to identify Jesus with a kiss. Judas's willingness to betray Jesus's trust and give in to temptation provided Satan with the access he needed to interfere with God's plan.

Herod the Great was deeply disturbed when he learned of the birth of a Messiah, perceiving it as a direct threat to his rule. In response, he ordered the massacre of all male children aged two years and under in Bethlehem. Years later after Herod the Great's death, his son Herod Antipas—ruler of Galilee —played a pivotal role in the execution of John the Baptist.

> ^{21} *Finally the opportune time came. On his birthday Herod*
> *gave a banquet for his high officials and military*
> *commanders and the leading men of Galilee.*
> **Mark 6:21 (NIV)**

Herod's birthday became the opportune time for the violent tendencies associated with his family history of trying to murder the prophets of God to surface. Herod had previously imprisoned John the Baptist for publicly criticizing his marriage to Herodias, his brother's wife. During his birthday celebration, Herod promised to grant his daughter any wish she desired. At her mother's urging, she requested the head of John the Baptist. Influenced by this request and the promise he had made, Herod ordered John's execution and presented his head to his daughter. Familiar spirit - a recurring destructive influence or pattern within a family line that can manifest in moments of vulnerability or crisis, is seen in Herod's actions.

The devil is opportunistic—he looks for moments of vulnerability to exploit, enforcing every detail of any harmful spiritual agreement that we or our ancestors may have made with him. Even after the initiator of the covenant have passed away, the demonic spirit associated with that agreement—a familiar spirit—continues to enforce its power and making the bloodline pay causing ongoing struggles or setbacks within the bloodline.

However, glory to God, we have hope through a superior covenant: a new spiritual agreement sealed by the blood of Jesus Christ, which brings freedom, forgiveness, and restoration. This means that we have the authority, in Jesus' name, to break the power of any evil covenant and cast out any familiar spirit, using the power and authority Jesus has given us as believers we can begin a new legacy for ourselves and our family.

When Jesus had called the Twelve together, he gave them power and authority to drive out all demons and to cure diseases, ² and he sent them out to proclaim the kingdom of God and to heal the sick.
Luke 9:1-2 (NIV)

Ignorance does not typically invalidate a covenant. For example, when you finance or lease a car, you enter into a legally binding agreement with the dealership. Even if you didn't fully understand all the finance details, you are generally still responsible for making the monthly payments on time for the duration of the contract. If you fail to do so, the dealership can repossess the car and your credit will be damaged, making it difficult to finance another vehicle in the future.

Joshua and the Israelites were obligated to uphold their covenant with the Gibeonites, notwithstanding the fact that the agreement was established under deceptive circumstances.

¹⁴ The Israelites sampled their provisions but did not inquire of the Lord. ¹⁵ Then Joshua made a treaty of peace with them to let them live, and the leaders of the assembly ratified it by oath.

Joshua 9:14-15 (NIV)

An agreement established under deceptive circumstances proved sufficiently binding on Israel and their descendants that Israel could not raise their hands to strike the Gibeonites fearing that God's wrath might fall upon them if they violated the oath they made. Joshua then placed a curse on the Gibeonites for deceiving Israel.

²² Then Joshua summoned the Gibeonites and said, "Why did you deceive us by saying, 'We live a long way from you,' while actually you live near us? ²³ You are now under a curse: You will never be released from service as woodcutters and water carriers for the house of my God."
Joshua 9:22-23 (NIV)

Please read all of Joshua chapter 9 for more insight.

Be intentional about what you say yes to. Be quick to say no and slow to say yes because your yes signifies consent. Research before you say yes, practice praying before you agree to anything. It is true we are saved; our salvation has benefits that we should daily contend for – divine health, deliverance, peace, joy, prosperity, abundant life etc.

If you do not see these benefits in your life, contend for them now because:

¹² From the days of John the Baptist until now, the kingdom of heaven has been subjected to violence, and violent people have been raiding it.

Matthew 11:12 (NIV)

Raid the kingdom for what Jesus has already paid for. Healing is the children's bread, deliverance is the children's bread. Jesus taught us to ask God for our daily bread. The demon possessed boy was immediately healed when Jesus delivered him from the demon. Raid the kingdom of God for your healing, for your deliverance. This is the reason Jesus died. He became a curse for us upon that cross so that a curse can no longer alight on us.

Like a fluttering sparrow or a darting swallow,
an undeserved curse does not come to rest.
Proverbs 26:2 (NIV)

Once we repent and appropriate the work Jesus did on the cross, the curse become causeless, we no longer deserve the curse.

[13] Christ redeemed us from the curse of the law by becoming a curse for us, for it is written: "Cursed is everyone who is hung on a pole."
Galatians 3:13 (NIV)

Jesus took our place on that cross, he took the curse meant for us, took the death penalty that we deserved and to sweeten the deal he cancelled our debts and every satanic legal demands. In-your-face devil.

14 having canceled out the certificate of debt consisting of legal demands [which were in force] against us and which

were hostile to us. And this certificate He has set
aside and completely removed by nailing it to the cross.
[15] When He had disarmed the rulers and authorities [those
supernatural forces of evil operating against us], He made a
public example of them [exhibiting them as captives in His
triumphal procession], having triumphed over them
through the cross.
Colossians 2:14-15 (Amp)

Hallelujah, we have the power to break every evil covenant made by us or for us with its legal demands because Jesus nailed them on the cross. He became the curse for us, and He disarmed our enemy (the evil forces operating against us, the familiar spirits, the accuser of the brethren) by His blood and through His death He triumphed over them. We are victorious.

If you are new to fasting, you can start from 6am to 12 noon and then work your way up. Pick a day in the week, be consistent with it, make it a habit and before you know it becomes easier to turn down your plate to seek God's face. If you are wondering what you should do while fasting. Start by reading Isaiah 58, It lets us know the type of fasting that God has chosen.

Is this not the fast that I have chosen: To loose the bonds of
wickedness, To undo the heavy burdens, To let the
oppressed go free, And that you break every yoke? [7] Is it not
to share your bread with the hungry,
And that you bring to your house the poor who are cast out;
When you see the naked, that you cover him, And not hide
yourself from your own flesh?
Isaiah 58:6-7 (NIV)

This is the fast that is acceptable to God: forgive, God forgives our debts as we forgive our debtors.

²⁵ And when you stand praying, if you hold anything against anyone, forgive them, so that your Father in heaven may forgive you your sins. "
Mark 11:25 (NIV)

Letting go of grievance is more beneficial for you than for them. They were wicked to you, yet you must free them from their wrongness to be freed from yours. I recall Pastor Stephanie Ike Okafor's insightful comment regarding perseverance in well doing; she emphasized that we do not reap from whom we have sown, but rather, we reap what we have sown. This perspective had a significant impact on me. I was able to let go of the person I poured all my energy and love into that had betrayed my trust. I focused on what I sowed, not on whom I sowed into. I had initially said in my heart that I would never open myself to be hurt and broken again. But if we stop sowing love, joy, mercy, forgiveness, goodness, we will not receive those back. If we stop expecting those back from the people we sowed into, we release ourselves to receive those things from God.

⁹ Let us not become weary in doing good, for at the proper time we will reap a harvest if we do not give up.
Galatians 6:9 (NIV)

Finally, give to the poor when you are fasting.

Whoever is kind to the poor lends to the Lord,
and he will reward them for what they have done.
Proverbs 19:17 (NIV)

Fasting is a discipline that challenges our physical comfort. With consistent practice, it becomes progressively easier to refrain from gratifying the desires of the flesh and to live a surrendered life characterized by self-discipline.

5. ***We develop a disciplined life by living a life of obedience.***

[7] So submit to [the authority of] God. Resist the devil [stand firm against him] and he will flee from you.
James 4:7 (AMP)

Submit is the Greek word **hypotasso** meaning to be under obedience. When we submit or obey God, we are giving consent for His will to be done in our lives. We are giving Him rule, reign and dominion. A life submitted to God is a life that can stand firm against the enemy. When we are in full submission to God, there is no room for the enemy, he has to flee. There are provision, protection, reward and power in our obedience to God. In 1 Samuel 15 Saul, Israel's first king was commanded by God to utterly destroy the Amalekites.

Samuel said to Saul, "I am the one the Lord sent to anoint you king over his people Israel; so listen now to the message from the Lord. 2 This is what the Lord Almighty

says: 'I will punish the Amalekites for what they did to Israel when they waylaid them as they came up from Egypt. 3 Now go, attack the Amalekites and totally destroy all that belongs to them. Do not spare them; put to death men and women, children and infants, cattle and sheep, camels and donkeys.'" 9 But Saul and the army spared Agag and the best of the sheep and cattle, the fat calves and lambs—everything that was good. These they were unwilling to destroy completely, but everything that was despised and weak they totally destroyed.
1 Samuel15: 1-3&9 (NIV)

Saul went to war with the Amalekites, he defeated and destroyed Amalekites, but he spared their king and the best of the sheep and of the cattle and of the fatlings, and the lambs, and all that was valuable, he destroyed the weak and the despised. He did not fully carry out the directive as instructed; rather, he selectively adhered to certain aspects of the command while disregarding others. God's command demands full obedience not selective obedience or delayed obedience.

Have you ever wondered why God rejected him as king if he only committed partial obedience? Why did God take a strong stance against King Saul? Understanding God's response requires looking back at both Saul's actions and Samuel's reaction, which reveal deeper reasons behind this pivotal decision. Samuel grieved for King Saul, hoping for a different outcome, but God did not relent. Instead, He rejected Saul as king and gave the Kingdom of Israel to David in his place. To grasp the significance of this event, let's review the back story and the events that took place about 300+ years before Saul's birth.

In Exodus 17 when Israel left Egypt and were camped at Rephidim, the Amalekites ambushed them with a surprise attack when they were vulnerable and weary. The Amalekites aggression prompted God's declaration against them. This led to the battle in which Moses kept his hands raised during Israel's conflict with the Amalekites, resulting in Joshua and the Israelites overcoming their opponents. This was Israel's first battle as a free nation on their way to the promise land. The Lord then made an oath in verse 14-16 (AMP):

> *14 Then the LORD said to Moses, "Write this in the book as a memorial and recite it to Joshua, that I will utterly wipe out the memory of Amalek [and his people] from under heaven." 15 And Moses built an altar and named it The LORD Is My Banner; 16 saying, "The LORD has sworn [an oath]; the LORD will have war against [the people of] Amalek from generation to generation."*

The LORD had made a promise to Moses that He would **utterly** wipe out Amalek from the face of the earth. He asked Moses to write it down as a memorial and to make sure Joshua heard it. Moses went a step further to build an alter to commemorate the oath God made to hold God to His word – building an altar was a way to mark significant encounters with God and to serve as a lasting reminder for future generations. Then in Deuteronomy 25:17-19 (NIV), the children of Israel were reminded not to forget what Amalekites did:

¹⁷ Remember what the Amalekites did to you along the way when you came out of Egypt. ¹⁸ When you were weary and worn out, they met you on your journey and attacked all who were lagging behind; they had no fear of God. ¹⁹ When the Lord your God gives you rest from all the enemies around you in the land he is giving you to possess as an inheritance, you shall blot out the name of Amalek from under heaven. Do not forget!

God commanded them to completely destroy Amalekites when they had settled in the promise land. Not only did King Saul disobey God, but he also broke the oath God made to his ancestors hundreds of years before his birth.

When God gives us a directive or a command to carry out, most times we may not be privy to the back story of that assignment. It sometimes may have something to do with someone else's assignment or a promise He made to someone else. While Jesus was on earth, He told His disciples that His bread was to do the will of His father. He carried out His assignment even becoming obedient to death. Everything Jesus did was not in isolation, every move He made was in fulfilment of scripture. God made a promise to the woman that her seed will crush the head of the serpent, Jesus not only crushed it, but He also nailed it.

Our assignments from God are never in isolation, it can impact a town, city, county, nation, a generation. Let us heed the words of 1Samuel 15:22b (NIV),

---

*To obey is better than sacrifice,
and to heed is better than the fat of rams.*

6. *We develop a disciplined life by resisting the devil.*

[7] So submit to [the authority of] God. Resist the devil [stand firm against him] and he will flee from you. [8] Come close to God [with a contrite heart] and He will come close to you.
James 4:7-8b (AMP)

Resist is the Greek work **anthistemi** – to stand against, to oppose, to withstand, to set oneself against. To oppose means to disagree with it and to actively work against it or stand in its way. When we oppose, stand against the devil (Satan, the false accuser) he will run away or vanish.

When Baalam was heading out to curse Israel, the angel of God came and stood in his way. Numbers 22:32 (NASB) says,

[32] Then the angel of the Lord said to him, "Why have you struck your donkey these three times? Behold, I have come out as an adversary, because your way was reckless and contrary to me.

Adversary is the Hebrew word **satan** meaning opponent, adversary, one who withstands, the arch-enemy of good. The angel of the Lord intervened as an adversary to Balaam, seeking to halt his efforts to pronounce a curse upon God's people. The angel stood in his path to oppose him, to withstand him but Balaam persisted in his mission. He would not turn back, he pushed forward. God had to open the donkey's mouth to speak to Balaam to stop him in his tracks. Balaam engaged in a conversation with his donkey as if it were a commonplace occurrence. In such a situation, I would likely have dismounted and ran in the opposite direction. To resist the devil means to oppose the opposer or to stand against the one whose job is to withstand you.

♦ *To resist the devil is to flip the script on the enemy, to beat him at his own game.*

Satan expects us to cower in fear. When he comes in like a flood remember that the Spirit of the Lord will lift up a standard against him and put him to flight (Isaiah 59:19). We waste precious time fleeing from our adversary who should be fleeing from us. The devil is going to come to oppose us even when we are living an uncompromising holy life. So, we might as well suit up with the armor of God, get ready for battle with an offensive stance and withstand him. We can maintain a steadfast and resolute posture, remaining firm in our convictions without yielding to external influences, yielding only to the will of God.

In 1 Chronicles chapter 21, Satan the adversary came to oppose David and incited him to sin against God. David did not resist him, and his action brought a considerable amount of grief upon Israel.

21 Satan [the adversary] stood up against Israel and incited David to count [the population of] Israel.

. ² So David said to Joab and the commanders of the troops, "Go and count the Israelites from Beersheba to Dan. Then report back to me so that I may know how many there are."

"³ But Joab replied, "May the Lord multiply his troops a hundred times over. My lord the king, are they not all my lord's subjects? Why does my lord want to do this? Why should he bring guilt on Israel?"

⁴ The king's word, however, overruled Joab; so Joab left and went throughout Israel and then came back to Jerusalem. ⁵ Joab reported the number of the fighting men to David: In all Israel there were one million one hundred thousand men who could handle a sword, including four hundred and seventy thousand in Judah.

⁶ But Joab did not include Levi and Benjamin in the numbering, because the king's command was repulsive to him. ⁷ This command was also evil in the sight of God; so he punished Israel.
1 Chronicles 21:1-6 (NIV)

To incite means to entice or to seduce. To seduce means to attract someone to a belief or into a course of action that is inadvisable or foolhardy – recklessly bold or rash. Was the census inherently sinful? Probably not, in the past God had instructed Moses to count Israel in Exodus 30 so we know it is not. So why was it a sin against God for David to count Israel? Is it because God did not command it like He did with Moses? In Moses case he was commanded to have the counted men pay a ransom.

[11] Then the Lord said to Moses, [12] "When you take the census of the Israelites, each one shall give a ransom for himself to the Lord when you count them, so that no plague will come on them when you number them.
Exodus 30:11-12 (NIV)

The ransom or price for a life was half a shekel and was considered a contribution to the service of the tent of meeting. It was an atonement money that brought about reconciliation, forgiveness, cleansing, mercy, pardon and prevented the plague from coming upon them.

David ordered the census of Israel following great victories from God over the Ammonites and Philistines, as described in 1 Chronicles chapters 19 and 20. God did not command the census, there was no atonement done to prevent the plague. David's own military commander tried to dissuade him, but David prevailed in his quest. The punishment was dire for Israel – three days of the sword of the Lord and plague in the land, with the angel of the Lord bringing destruction throughout all the territory of Israel.

[11] So Gad went to David and said to him, "This is what the Lord says: 'Take your choice: [12] three years of

famine, three months of being swept away before your enemies, with their swords overtaking you, or three days of the sword of the Lord—days of plague in the land, with the angel of the Lord ravaging every part of Israel.' Now then, decide how I should answer the one who sent me." ¹³ David said to Gad, "I am in deep distress. <u>Let me fall into the hands of the Lord, for his mercy is very great; but do not let me fall into human hands</u>."

14 So the Lord sent a plague on Israel, and 70,000 men of Israel fell. 15 God sent an angel to Jerusalem to destroy it; and as he was destroying it, the Lord looked and relented concerning the catastrophe and said to the destroying angel, "It is enough; now remove your hand [of judgment]."
1 Chronicles 21:11-15 (AMP)

As the destroyer was ravaging Israel with death the Lord looked and relented – He was moved to pity and compassion, He was sorry just like David had anticipated that He would because of His mercy. God said to the destroyer "enough, withdraw (cease, drop) your hand (terror, custody, debt, strength)."

God not only relented but He made provision for us - His people to escape destruction Isaiah 54:

¹⁶ *"Listen carefully, I have created the smith who blows on the fire of coals*
And who produces a weapon for its purpose; And I have created the destroyer to inflict ruin.
¹⁷ *"No weapon that is formed against you will succeed;*
Isaiah 54:16-17a(AMP)

---

but no weapon that can hurt you has ever been forged.
Isaiah 54:17a (MSG)

I created the destroyer – *sahat* meaning spoiler, waster, corrupter, destroyer to inflict ruin (to pervert, to bind, to writhe in pain, travail), no weapon that the destroyer can use against you will succeed or achieve it's intended purpose. We have the power to stop the destroyer, to say enough withdraw your hand. Satan, our adversary is not our friend. He withstands and makes accusations against us to bring us destruction like he did to Joshua the high priest in Zechariah 3: 1-2 (AMP):

¹Then the guiding angel showed me Joshua the high priest [representing disobedient, sinful Israel] standing before the Angel of the Lord, and Satan standing at Joshua's right hand to be his adversary and to accuse him. ²And the Lord said to Satan, "The Lord rebuke you, Satan! Even the Lord, who [now and ever] has chosen Jerusalem, rebuke you! Is this not a log snatched and rescued from the fire?"

And he continues to accuse us before God day and night with a record of all the sins we have committed:

¹⁰Then I heard a loud voice in heaven, saying, "Now the salvation, and the power, and the kingdom (dominion, reign) of our God, and the authority of His Christ have come; for the accuser of our [believing] brothers and sisters has been thrown down [at last], he who accuses them and keeps bringing charges [of sinful behavior] against them before our God day and night.
Revelations 12:10 (AMP)

But our God has also made a provision for us to counter the accusations of the adversary. Isaiah 54:17b says,

And every tongue that rises against you in judgment you will condemn.
This [peace, righteousness, security, and triumph over opposition] is the heritage of the servants of the Lord,
And this is their vindication from Me," says the Lord. (AMP)

Any accuser who takes you to court
will be dismissed as a liar.
This is what God's servants can expect.
I'll see to it that everything works out for the best."
God's Decree. (MSG)

Every tongue (language, evil speaker, flame, fire, babbler, talker, wedge) that rises against us in judgment (to bring a suit, a charge, a case, a sentence, an order against us), we shall condemn (declare wicked, guilty, to disturb, violate, condemn, make trouble). This is our inheritance (portion) as servants of the Lord.

What is the tongue that has risen against you in judgement? Condemn it, declare it guilty. Exodus 22 tells us that anyone that is found guilty must pay back double. Declare the tongue guilty that has risen against you in judgement, it must pay back double. Give the devil no room. He is like a roaring lion looking for whom to devour. You give him an inch; he takes a foothold which then turns into a stronghold that would require you to destroy its fruit above the ground and its root below the ground. If you see the fruit of the enemy in your life, look for the root below the ground and destroy it (Amos 2:9). While men slept – *katheudo* meaning are while men were indifferent to their salvation or yielded to sloth and sin is when the adversary came in to sow tares - false grain (Matthew 13:25). Wake up oh sleeper and Christ will shine upon you *and* give you light that brings illumination. God has appointed us as watchmen. A watchman keeps guard and controls access to a place.

⁶ On your walls, Jerusalem, I have placed sentries; They must never be silent day or night.
They must remind the Lord of his promises And never let him forget them.
⁷ They must give him no rest until he restores Jerusalem And makes it a city the whole world praises.
Isaiah 62:6-7 (GNT)

As watchmen, our duty is to speak up, daily remind God of His promises, and persistently seek His attention. When we take the stance of a watchman over our family, the enemy has got to pass through us first before he can get to our children or spouse. There is no passivity in this Christendom. We the righteous are bold like lions; lions are never passive. Caleb went to battle with the fighting men at eighty-five years old, he was as vigorous as he was at forty years old. He did not back down, he stood his ground and laid claim to the inheritance that God promised him.

We have grown accustomed to taking a defensive stand against our common enemy but what if we switched to actively opposing him? What would that look like? This poem is for the warrior in you.

Warrior

I see a man bound and surrounded
The enemy pulls the bands to keep him down
Each time he makes a move
His adversary tightens his hold
He is weary, his back is drenched with sweat
He's about ready to quit the game
The angels watch with bated breath, he sees His savior
With nail marked hands he beckons him forward
He locks eyes with Him, takes one step forward and another
Every step stretches the bands
And another
The bands tighten, dig into his flesh
And another
The bands draw blood and snap
With each painful step
he gains ground,
He gains freedom, he gains momentum
The great unseen cloud of witnesses cheers him on
He continues resisting
With each step moving forward
He becomes stronger, becomes buffer
His opponent becomes frantic as he loses his hold
With a grin on his face, he shakes off all bands, walks out
free
His adversary flees
The angels provide succor
He smiles at his savior, looks at his scars
A clear reminder of where he's been
He dusts himself and tells all it was worth it.

Therefore, since we are surrounded by so great a cloud of witnesses [who by faith have testified to the truth of God's absolute faithfulness], stripping off every unnecessary weight and the sin which so easily and cleverly entangles us, let us run with endurance and active persistence the race that is set before us,
Hebrews 12:1 (AMP)

We have taken the devil's beat down long enough. It is time to resist him not in our own flesh but with all the weapons that Jesus gave us for spiritual warfare. This is not for the faint-hearted. This is for the bold believers who are sick and tired of being sick and tired. It is time to, say it out loud: "Resist."

Daily Confession: Today is the day I choose to stand against, to oppose, to withstand, to set myself against the kingdom of darkness with my words, my thoughts, and with my actions by so doing I take territories for God.

CHAPTER SEVEN

REASON FOR THE SEASONS

*"All scripture is given by inspiration of God, and is profitable for doctrine, for reproof, for correction, for instruction in righteousness: ¹⁷ That the man of God may be **perfect, thoroughly furnished unto all good works.***

2 Timothy 3:16-17 (KJV)

All four seasons work together to perfect us, to thoroughly furnish us unto all good works. The Greek word for perfect is the word **artios** meaning fitted, complete. The definition of complete is to make something whole. A whole person is unbroken, undamaged, in one piece, complete in itself.

*¹⁷ That the man of God may be perfect (artios – complete), **thoroughly furnished** unto all good works.*
2 Timothy 3:16-17(KJV)

Exartizo is the Greek word for thoroughly furnished meaning to equip fully, complete, finish, accomplish. God uses the four seasons to perfect us, to make us whole and to accomplish or finish His work through us. All He needs is our obedience. Our obedience is our consent for Him to do His will through us on this earth as it is in heaven.

*²⁰ Now may the God of peace [the source of serenity and spiritual well-being] who brought up from the dead our Lord Jesus, the great Shepherd of the sheep, through the blood that sealed and ratified the eternal covenant, ²¹ **equip** you with every good thing to carry out His will and strengthen you [making you complete and perfect as you ought to be], accomplishing in us that which is pleasing in His sight, through Jesus Christ, to whom be the glory forever and ever. Amen.*

Hebrews 13:20-21(AMP)

Katartizo is the Greek word for equip in this verse meaning to render fit, sound, to complete thoroughly, mend what has been broken or rent, to repair, to perfectly join, restore.

Let's look at these two Greek words that mean equip deeper – **exartizo vs katartizo**. I believe that the word *exartizo* deals with equipping a vessel that is whole, nothing missing, nothing broken for good works. God accomplishes His work through this vessel, completes and perfects it. While k*artartizo* deals with equipping and strengthening a broken vessel to carry out the will of God. God must restore, make sound, mend what has been broken, repair it first and then accomplish his perfect work through this vessel.

katartizo *is for anyone wondering, "Can God still use me after I've failed, made mistakes and let Him down?"*

If you feel you've made mistakes, God can still mend what's broken if you let Him do a katartizo – repair work within you. He can put you back together again and when he does, you will be perfect, complete, whole and furnished for good work. He alone can turn your ashes into beauty.

> [22] *Cast your burden on the Lord,*
> *And He shall sustain you;*
> *He shall never permit the righteous to be <u>moved</u>.*
> **Psalm 55:22 (NKJV)**

The Hebrew word for moved is **mot.** One of its meanings is to be out of course. If you cast your burdens to God, He will make provision for you and course correct you if you turn back to Him. Remember Rahab, the prostitute – she is in the lineage of Jesus. David the man after God's own heart committed adultery and murdered the husband, he is also in Jesus's lineage. We may have some cracks, but His grace is the glue that holds us together until the coming of Christ. Our scars serve as a testimony of where we've been and the power of God to restore, they speak for us. Out of ashes God makes beauty, we are beautiful with our scars and all.

> ❖ *God did not just call us to do good works by ourselves, He equips us, thoroughly furnishes us for our assignment.*

What assignment?

2 Timothy 3:17, a perfect (complete, whole) man of God (that is you and I) is equipped unto all good works. **Ergon** is the Greek word for works meaning business, employment, that

which one undertakes to do, any product whatever, anything accomplished by hand, art, industry, or mind, occupation.

We all have an assignment, a work, calling on our lives right before the womb. How do I know this?

"Before I formed you in the womb I knew you [and approved of you as My chosen instrument], And before you were born I consecrated you [to Myself as My own];
I have appointed you as a prophet to the nations."
Jeremiah 1:5 (AMP)

⁴just as He chose us in Him before the foundation of the world, that we should be holy and without blame before Him in love,
Ephesians 1:4 (NKJV)

Katabole is the Greek word for foundation, and it means conception, throwing or laying down, the injection or depositing of virile semen in the womb. Before we were conceived, God picked us, selected us, chose us to be set apart and unblameable before Him in love. That should make us feel special and loved.

Without Christ, we go through life with blinders, groping and stumbling in darkness without clear guidance. It is the devil's plan for us to stay that way and never come into the fullness of who we were created to be. However, everything changes when we encounter Jesus Christ, we wake up to the reality that we are the called, "a chosen generation, a royal priesthood, a holy nation, God's special possession, that you may declare the praises of him who called you out of darkness into his wonderful light", (1 Peter 2:9)

¹⁰ For we are God's handiwork, created in Christ Jesus to do good <u>works</u>, which God prepared in advance for us to do.
Ephesians 2:10 (NIV)

Works in this verse is the same Greek word **ergon** that was used in 2 Timothy 3:17 that means business, employment, that which one undertakes to do, any product whatever, anything accomplished by hand, art, industry, or mind, occupation. Not only did God choose us before we were conceived, but He also prepared our work beforehand, from eternity. I have heard some individuals express that their work aligns closely with their sense of purpose, that it feels like what they were born to do. That is because our work was ordained before we got here, and they are good works.

Both scriptures called our works good which is the Greek word **agathos** meaning excellent, honorable, useful, joyful, happy. We each have different assignments, you may be called to be a stay home mom, a preacher, a truck driver, doctor, lawyer etc. Regardless of your specific assignment, do not minimize the impact it will have on this world instead recognize its significance. Your assignment, your work is agathos - it is excellent, honorable, useful, joyful, happy. So, use it to declare the praises of Him who called you. We are not called in isolation, we are called in community. We need each other.

Genesis chapter 1 lets us know that God made us in his image and likeness – a resemblance of Himself. The united trinity made a tripartite man –consisting of three parts. We - our body, soul and spirit were created perfectly as a whole - complete in itself and in one piece. A whole complete man walked in oneness with the God of creation in the garden of Eden. Disobedience to the directive given by God brought spiritual death to man. The serpent deceived Eve by telling her that she would be like God if she ate from the Tree of the knowledge of good and evil, not realizing that she was already like God she obeyed the serpent.

Adam and Eve obedience to the devil gave him consent to take over their authority on the earth but God made provision to restore our relationship with Him and to give us back our authority and dominion, to put us back together through the wonderful powerful cross of Jesus.

> [23] *May God himself, the God of peace, sanctify you through and through. May your whole spirit, soul and body be kept blameless at the coming of our Lord Jesus Christ.*
> ***1 Thessalonians 5:23(NIV)***

Only the God of peace can sanctify us – make us holy and keep us whole. We cannot attain holiness by own effort. Trust me, I have tried and failed miserably. The Greek word for keep is **tereo** means to attend to carefully, to hold fast, to take care of, to guard properly by keeping the eye upon. If man gave into sin, while living in the garden of Eden undistracted, it makes sense that God would want to guard us who are heirs of salvation jealously and hold us fast until the coming of Christ. It did cost Him His only son to bring us back into unity with Himself. We are too precious to God and He made sure to tell us so in Isaiah 43:4 (NIV),

[4] Since you are precious (costly, valuable, esteemed) and honored in my sight, and because I love you, I will give people in exchange for you, nations in exchange for your life.

God started us whole – unbroken in the Garden of Eden and He is coming back for a church without spot, and wrinkle, a holy unblemished church. It will take total surrender and a free fall into God's will for us to see His keeping power at work in our lives. A life that is free from sin cannot be accomplished by our own power and might but by the Spirit of God.

"we have this precious treasure [the good news about salvation] in [unworthy] earthen vessels [of human frailty], so that the grandeur and surpassing greatness of the power will be [shown to be] from God [His sufficiency] and not from ourselves"
2 Corinthians 4:7 (AMP)

Wholeness is not a destination. It is a journey. Our daily surrender to God's will and purpose allows Him to do a work of sanctification in us to make us whole. Paul said it best in Philippians 3:13-14 (MSG):

12-14 I'm not saying that I have this all together, that I have it made. But I am well on my way, reaching out for Christ, who has so wondrously reached out for me. Friends, don't get me wrong: By no means do I count myself an expert in all of this, but I've got my eye on the goal, where God is beckoning us onward—to Jesus. I'm off and running, and I'm not turning back.

Keep running child of God toward the mark of the high calling of God in Christ Jesus and don't look back.

CHAPTER EIGHT

CONCLUSION

Solomon, the wisest man that ever lived said in Ecclesiastes 12:13 (NIV):

Let us hear the conclusion of the whole matter: Fear God, and keep his commandments: for this is the whole duty of man.

When it is all said and done, the totality of our duty is to reverence and obey God. For every season that we go through, He makes Himself available to guide and to guard His own. There is a reason for every season, there are opportunities to pluck and territories to take. If a season makes you cry, then cry, let it all out. Your tears are not wasted; God has your tears.

[8] You have taken account of my wanderings;
Put my tears in Your bottle.
Are they not recorded in Your book?

[9] Then my enemies will turn back in the day when I call;
This I know, that God is for me.
Psalm 56: 8-9 (AMP)

In summary, each "season" represents a distinct phase in our spiritual journey, marked by unique challenges and opportunities for growth. For example, the first season is a time of learning and preparation, where we focus on studying and storing the word in our heart—like a student beginning a new school year, eagerly absorbing new lessons. In the second season, our faith in the word is proved (tested) to examine its genuineness; just as a plant must weather storms to grow stronger, we face trials that test our commitment to what we've learned. Should we miss the mark or are overcome by temptation, the third season of correction facilitates rectification and personal restoration— imagine an athlete recovering from injury, receiving care and guidance to get back on track.

Finally, in the season of instruction, we sit at the feet of the Holy Spirit in His school, receiving ongoing training in righteousness. It's a time of continual growth, drawing us ever closer to reflecting God's character. We are guided towards virtuous living and encouraged to exemplify spiritual principles in our daily lives.

We are all at different seasons in our walk with the Lord, so it is important to be understanding and to extend grace to one another. The duration of a season is determined by our willingness to surrender to God's will. Progressing to the subsequent season requires successfully completing the current one and understanding its intended lessons and purposes.

Are the seasons experienced in sequential order? Not necessarily. But in my own walk with God, I noticed that I have gone through these seasons in a consecutive order. When I started writing this book I was in the season of Reproof in Righteousness. As I approached the conclusion of this book, I entered the season of Instruction (training) in Righteousness.

What season are you in, and what has God shown or taught you during your journey with Him? Let's continue this conversation with our friends and family and encourage each other through our seasons of life.

To sum it all up in the words of Apostle Paul in 2 Timothy 4:6-8:

"You take over. I'm about to die, my life an offering on God's altar. This is the only race worth running. I've run hard right to the finish, believed all the way. All that's left now is the shouting—God's applause! Depend on it, he's an honest judge. He'll do right not only by me, but by everyone eager for his coming. (MSG)"

This is a word for your season; God bless you now and always.

DELIVERANCE PRAYER

Step 1: Repentance

[14] if my people, who are called by my name, will humble themselves and pray and seek my face and turn from their wicked ways, then I will hear from heaven, and I will forgive their sin and will heal their land.

2 Chronicles 7:14

Turn down your plate and repent for any agreement you made with the devil, it could be your obedience to him that opened a door giving him legal access into your life. It could also be an agreement that your ancestors or your parents made with the enemy. You can repent on their behalf. Read Daniel chapter 9 as an example of how to repent for something you did not do that affected you.

Step 2: Break the evil covenant.

I thank you LORD my God for forgiving our sins and for cleansing us from all unrighteousness with the blood of Jesus. I arise now as a bloodline breach repairer, and I break every evil covenant made by my ancestors and myself with -- ------------. I renounce and denounce these evil covenants. Jesus took every handwriting and legal demands against us and nailed them on the cross. I place the cross between me and these evil covenants, I place the cross between my spouse, my children, my bloodline and these evil covenants. I break these evil covenants with the blood of Jesus in the name of Jesus. I break them off my life, my children, my spouse and my bloodline. I disassociate myself, my children, my spouse and my bloodline from these evil covenants and we come out of agreement with them right now in Jesus name.

I renew the covenant I made with you God when I accepted Jesus as my Lord and Savior. A covenant sealed with the blood of Jesus that speaks a better word than the blood of Abel. I release the powerful blood of Jesus over myself and all that belongs to me. By this blood I and my household are exempted from disaster. We are delivered, redeemed, justified, healed, saved and protected. We have overcome by the blood of Jesus and by the word of our testimony. The covenant we have in Christ is superior to these broken evil covenants, so every agreement with the spirit of --------------------- is dismantled and annulled In Jesus name. I demolish your demonic stronghold; I close every door that gives you legal access. I silence every evil sacrifice made to you with the blood of Jesus; I silence and dismantle your demonic alter with the blood of Jesus. In Jesus name

Step 3: Cast out the evil spirit that was given access through the evil covenant.

Jesus, you gave me the power and authority to cast out evil spirits and to heal disease. Whatsoever I disallow on earth is disallowed in heaven. Based on the authority I have in the name of Jesus I bind you spirit of ----------------- and I cast you out of my life, out of my spouse, out of my children, out of my bloodline. I cast you into the abyss and I command you to never return to my life, my spouse's life, my children's life and to our bloodline. I rebuke you familiar spirit that has been enforcing these evil covenants in my bloodline, the evil covenants are broken, and you have no more legal ground or access to my life. I disarm you powers and principalities and

I triumph over you by the cross of Jesus Christ. I disallow you evils spirits from ever returning and operating in my life, my spouse's life, my children's life and my bloodline. I give the Holy Spirit reign, rule and dominion over my life, my spouse's life, my children's life and my bloodline in Jesus name,

Step 4: Break the curse –

covenants bring blessings or curses depending on whom the covenant was made with. Covenant with God bring blessings, covenant with the devil bring curses.

Lord Jesus, you became a curse for me when you died on the cross, it is written a curse causeless shall not alight in my life, my spouse's life, my children's life and my bloodline. I arise and break every and all associated curses that came into my life, my spouse's life, my children's life and my bloodline through these broken evil covenants. With the blood of Jesus I destroy their fruit above ground and their roots below ground (Amos 2:9). I break the curse of anti-marriage, divorce, premature death, delays, disappointments, rejection, isolation, incest, molestation, infidelity, abortion, fornication, sexual sins, disobedience, rebellion, hardship, poverty, infirmity, genetic disease, infertility, barrenness etc. I sanitize my life, my spouse's life, my children's life and my bloodline with the blood of Jesus and I wash away the residue of these curses with the blood of Jesus in Jesus name.

Step 5: Replace with blessings.

Father it is written in your word that blessed is the man whose sins you have forgiven. I ask that you bless me, my spouse, my children and my bloodline, enlarge our territory, may your hand be upon us that we may not cause pain (1

Chronicles 4:10) instead let the sounds of joy and gladness be heard in my family. Lord restore our fortunes like you restored the streams of the Negev (Psalm 126:4 NIV). Restore the years the cankerworms stole from us (Joel 2:25) – restore marriages, favor, finances, peace, joy, laughter, health, wisdom, restore us to our rightful minds, restore destinies, restore our youth, restore all these speedily.

We worship you Lord our God, according to Exodus 23:25 may your blessing be on your food and water, take away sickness from among us, do not allow anyone to miscarry or be barren in our land and give us a full life span in Jesus name. According to Isaiah 65 from verse 20 I declare that never again will there be in our bloodline an infant who lives but a few days, or an old man who does not live out his years; the one who dies at a hundred will be thought a mere child; the one who fails to reach a hundred will be considered accursed. We will build houses and dwell in them; we will plant vineyards and eat their fruit. No longer will we build houses and others live in them, or plant and others eat. For as the days of a tree, so will be the days of our bloodline; we your chosen ones will long enjoy the work of our hands. We will not labor in vain, nor will we bear children doomed to misfortune; for we will be a people blessed by the Lord, us and our descendants with us. [24] Before we call You will answer; while we are still speaking God, You will hear us in Jesus name"

Step 6. – Praise God and end with communion.

Remember to maintain your deliverance by not giving the devil any foothold that would allow him to return to your life. God bless you all.

It is for freedom that Christ has set us free. Stand firm, then, and do not let yourselves be burdened again by a yoke of slavery. Galatians 5:1 (NIV)

Author Contact

Joyjoshua.com